Ensuring Success in Math and Science

Curriculum and
Teaching Strategies
for At-Risk Learners

Solution Tree

Randolf Tobias

GRADES K–8

Copyright © 2007 by Solution Tree
(formerly National Educational Service)
304 West Kirkwood Avenue
Bloomington, IN 47404–5131
(812) 336–7700
FAX: (812) 336–7790
email: info@solution-tree.com
www.solution-tree.com

Cover design by Grannan Graphic Design Ltd.

Printed in the United States of America

ISBN 978-1-932127-88-1

Dedication

To my wife, Sandye, who has nurtured an environment in which my collection of thoughts could ultimately become a published volume.

Acknowledgments

I would like to express sincere thanks to my colleague Velma Hill, lecturer in mathematics at York College of the City University of New York, not only for her contribution to the content of chapters 6 and 7, but also for her creative development of activities accompanying most of the lesson plans. Ms. Hill is also responsible for the list of websites where students and their families can obtain information about math and science reinforcement activities (see Appendix B, page 181). A note of thanks is also due to various faculty and personnel within the math and math education departments of Queens College of the City University of New York, for answering my questions relative to the metric system and mathematical equations.

I also extend my appreciation to the former principal of public school 499 (Queens College School for Math, Science and Technology), Joseph J. Saccente, and the present principal, Anastasia Schneider, for allowing me to observe how children are taught within this wonderful school. Special thanks to Ms. Schneider, also, for accessing and sharing children's norm-referenced test data. Both Mr. Saccente and Ms. Schneider are former students of my classes in curriculum and school administration.

Special thanks to Diana Daniti, Margarita Dhandari, Diane Jellama, Jennifer Vigro, Keiko Shirata, Ms. Rabson, and Kendra Tomlinson. These wonderful teachers graciously allowed me to visit their classrooms and observe their teaching. Thank you, Amelia

Everett, parent coordinator, for organizing my class visitations and meetings with teachers to share results of my observations. I would also like to acknowledge my typist, Jeannie Butler, whose keen eye for editing as well as word processing is sincerely appreciated. Thank you, Jeannie. Finally, I thank my editor, Gretchen Knapp, and the staff at Solution Tree for all their work to support this book.

About the Authors

Randolf Tobias is an emeritus professor of Educational Leadership at Queens College of the City University of New York. His work on curriculum and teaching has been widely published. He is also the author of *Nurturing At-Risk Youth in Math and Science* (1992, Solution Tree [formerly National Educational Service]). Dr. Tobias has consulted nationally and internationally with school systems and universities on curriculum and teaching approaches to increase the learning potential of the educationally at risk. He resides in North Carolina and teaches at Belmont Abbey College.

Velma Hill is a lecturer in mathematics at York College of the City University of New York, and is finishing her doctoral dissertation in topology, an area of mathematics that analyzes the properties of geometric figures. She has received many teaching awards, including the Outstanding Woman in Mathematics Award and the Children's Service Mathematics Award. Ms. Hill specializes in teaching students who are weak in basic math and test-taking skills within the University Skills Emergence Program.

Table of Contents

Introduction 1

   A Turning Point in American Education 3

**PART 1: FUNDAMENTAL PROBLEMS AND LONG-RANGE
STRATEGIES** 9

**Chapter 1: Fundamental Problems Causing
Math and Science Failure** 11

   Insufficient Pre-Service Preparation of Teachers 11

   Insufficient Professional Development of Teachers 13

   Homogeneous Grouping and Tracking of Students 15

   Poor Preparation of Students for High School

      Math and Science 16

   Other Problems 17

      Standardized Testing 17

      Gender Inequity 18

      Technology 20

      Summary 21

Chapter 2: Long-Range Strategies 23

   Problem One: Insufficient Pre-Service Preparation 23

      State Departments of Education 24

        Strategy: Rubrics 25

      Colleges and Universities 26

        Strategy: Contextual Learning 26

        Strategy: Whole-Language Approach 29

Local School Districts 30
Strategy: Early Field Exposure 30
Problem Two: Insufficient Professional Development 33
Strategy: Action Research 34
Strategy: Educational Leadership 36
Problem Three: Homogenous Grouping and Tracking 38
Strategy: Inclusive Education 38
Problem Four: Poor Preparation for High School 39
Strategy: Correlates of Effective Schools 39
Summary 41

PART 2: SHORT-RANGE STRATEGIES 43
Chapter 3: Curriculum Redevelopment 45
Building Support for the Mission 46
Allocating Resources 46
Funding 46
Time 48
Human Resources 48
Space 49
Conducting a Needs Assessment 49
Item Analysis 49
Textbook Analysis 50
Teacher Observations 51
Developing Protocol Materials 54
Key Informant Surveys 54
Focus Groups 55
Modifying the Mission 57
Summary 58

Chapter 4: Curriculum Design 59
Conceptualizing the Curriculum 59
Organizing Instructional Programs 61
Including Scope, Sequence, Balance, and Integration 62

Designing Subject-, Learner-,
or Problem-Centered Curricula 65
Subject-Centered 65
Learner-Centered 65
Problem-Centered 67
Designing to Ensure Success for At-Risk Students 68
Interventions 68
Connections 69
Summary 71

Chapter 5: Curriculum Implementation 73
Sound Instructional Practice 73
Long-Range Thematic Planning 74
Teaching Skills and Strategies 76
The Problem-Solving Approach 77
Selection of Appropriate Supporting Materials
and Resources 78
Effective Classroom Management 78
Accurate Pupil Assessment 79
Professional Development 81
Beginning Teachers of Math and Science 81
Experienced Teachers of Math and Science 83
Summary 85

PART 3: CREATIVE TEACHING AND HOME REINFORCEMENT . . . 87

Chapter 6: Math and Science Lesson Plans That Work:
Early Education 89
With Velma Hill
Sample Mathematics Lesson Plan, Kindergarten 93
Sample Science Lesson Plan, Kindergarten 99
Sample Mathematics Lesson Plan, Grade 1 101
Sample Science Lesson Plan, Grade 1 107
Sample Mathematics Lesson Plan, Grade 2 109

Sample Integrated Mathematics and Science Lesson Plan,
Grade 3 111

**Chapter 7: Math and Science Lesson Plans That Work:
Elementary School** 117
With Velma Hill
Sample Mathematics Lesson Plan, Grade 4 119
Sample Science Lesson Plan, Grade 4 126
Sample Integrated Mathematics and Science Lesson Plan,
Grade 5 128

**Chapter 8: Math and Science Lesson Plans That Work:
Middle School** 135
With Velma Hill
Sample Mathematics Lesson Plan, Grade 6 136
Sample Science Lesson Plan, Grade 6 146
Sample Mathematics Lesson Plan, Grade 7 149
Sample Mathematics Lesson Plan, Grade 8 158

Chapter 9: The Role of Families and Care Providers 165
Using Math and Science at Home 166
Math Tasks 167
Science Tasks 168
Reinforcing School Lessons 169
Building Good Study Habits 170
Reducing Test Anxiety 170
Challenges for Families of At-Risk Students 171

Appendix A: Sample Science Unit Plan 173

Appendix B: Websites for Math and Science Reinforcement . . 181
Compiled by Velma Hill

References 185

Introduction

If someone had told me when I was in high school that one day I would write a book about helping students succeed in math and science, I would have been quite surprised. Back then, when I was a student in intermediate algebra, I struggled with math, like many students. But when I asked my teacher to spend some time with me after school to explain "balancing equations" and "getting rid of unknowns"—concepts that were not only unfamiliar, but intimidating—he gave a very curt and cold reply. He didn't have time. He had to get home before rush hour.

What was I to do? I felt quite abandoned. Then I remembered my friend Thomas Turner. His friends called him Tommy or just Thom. Math and science came naturally to Thom. He could ace those exams as easily as drinking a glass of cool water. I, on the other hand, would have to study past midnight to make a mere 70%. So I went, books in hand, to the park where Thom was practicing his basketball jump shot, and yelled, "Tommy! Can you explain this stuff to me?" That afternoon, Thom made all of my fears disappear, because he explained algebraic concepts using a language that I could understand.

But children shouldn't have to rely on their peers or even their parents to help them master these subjects. Their teachers must be able to explain math and science concepts and operations using language that demonstrates a relationship to the real world. When this kind of teaching demystifies math and science, children can connect math and science to their own daily lives. They lose their fear of these subjects and start to believe they can achieve success. As they engage with the subject, they develop the critical thinking skills so crucial to math and science mastery. This process of making connections to the real world is particularly important for children who are educationally at risk.

There is a pervasive cultural attitude in America that mathematics is abstract, difficult, and mastered by a select few. The American way of teaching math, which reduces mathematical concepts to a series of procedures to solve a problem, reflects this attitude (Allen, 2003). All too many children struggle with math and science as a result, and yet the extent to which today's children will succeed in the marketplace as adults depends upon their mastery of math, science, and computer technology. Mathematics and science "are the very areas from which the continued growth of the American economy will depend, and from which a high level of cognitive competence will be expected from its workers" (Armour-Thomas, 1992, p. 21). Children at risk are especially vulnerable to being left behind in this new economy.

Comer (1987) defines children at risk as those who underachieve despite intellectual endowment and, as a result, will underachieve as adults. Slavin (1989) states that a student described as at risk is in danger of failing to complete his or her education with an adequate level of skills. The six common denominators of the educationally at risk appear to be:

1. Academic underachievement

2. Poor school attendance

3. Low self-esteem

4. Negative attitudes toward school

5. Retention at grade level for 1 year or more

6. High dropout rates from school

Given these challenges, it is not surprising that these youngsters face more challenges achieving in math and science. But if schools can enable at-risk children to succeed in math and science, these six common denominators could virtually disappear.

A Turning Point in American Education

On November 27, 2000, Senator John Glenn, chairperson of the National Commission on Mathematics and Science Teaching for the 21st Century, issued a memorandum that commented on the inadequate math and science performance of American students:

> It is not that our schools, teachers, and students have declined. It is that other nations have become much better. They have seen the role of math and science in United States development and leadership, and are now out-educating us in this crucial area. (Glenn, 2000, p. 1)

This memorandum served as a cover letter to a more detailed report titled *Before It's Too Late: A Report to the Nation from the National Commission on Mathematics and Science Teaching for the 21st Century* (National Commission on Mathematics and Science Teaching for the 21st Century, 2000). The major findings in this report were as follows:

- The teaching pool in mathematics and science is inadequate to meet America's needs and includes many teachers who are unqualified or underqualified to teach these subject areas effectively. America's inability to attract and keep good teachers grows, and as a result of students receiving inadequate instruction, newer, technologically oriented industries have trouble finding enough qualified employees.

- At the fourth-grade assessment, American children scored among the leading performers of 41 nations participating in the Third International Mathematics and Science Study

(TIMSS). American eighth graders scored slightly above the international average in science and slightly below the international average in mathematics. By high school graduation, American students became almost the lowest performers.

- Recent assessments bear out the conclusions of the TIMSS: The longer American children are taught math and science, the less favorably they compare with their peers in other countries.

Math and science development during early childhood is crucial, particularly for African-American children. These children progress and thrive at the same rate as their Caucasian counterparts until the third grade (Kunjufu, 1985). After that point, unless they receive quality teaching, they begin a downward trend in learning. This poor transition between the primary and elementary levels is shown in a fourth-grade failure syndrome (Kunjufu, 1985). If they do not receive early remediation, at-risk children will suffer compounded math and science skill deficiency in upper-middle and high school.

Although other nations showed more successful results than the United States, the countries whose eighth graders received the highest scores in mathematics shared no common teaching method:

The National Center for Education Statistics analyzed 638 videotaped lessons [. . .] to determine whether high-performing countries share common teaching strategies. The lessons were taped in the U.S. and the six countries that scored higher on the [TIMSS] assessment: Australia, the Czech Republic, Hong Kong SAR, Japan, the Netherlands, and Switzerland.

The study looked at an array of variables including teacher backgrounds, lesson length, interruptions, procedural complexity, mathematical processes, and learning resources such as technology. Although the report found that teachers in high-scoring countries use similar teaching "ingredients," it concluded that each country combined instructional features in various ways, and no method could be recommended to predict success in a given country. (American Association of Colleges for Teacher Education, 2003, p. 1)

We still have much to learn from the methods used in high-scoring countries. Fortunately, American attitudes and teaching practices in math, science, and technology are slowly changing. The Association for Supervision and Curriculum Development maintains that math teachers across the country are now drawing from international expertise (Allen, 2003). American educators are learning, for example, that Japanese teachers allow students to struggle with a problem *before* they show students how to solve it. They are learning that the Singapore method teaches the computational functions of addition, subtraction, multiplication, and division *together,* rather than as separate units. These successful practices contradict American classroom practices, and American teachers are starting to revisit their traditional methodology as a result.

Science teaching is also changing. In many school districts, physics is now taught as early as the eighth grade, *before* chemistry and biology. This flip in the science sequence enables students to understand more deeply the concepts and connections across the sciences. Putting physics first has helped students to "enter chemistry class with a stronger understanding of atoms, and how these combine to form molecules, which, in turn, helps them with the complexities of modern biology" (Allen, 2004, p. 1).

In other changes, even though technology spending for schools has dropped in recent years, states have been able to maintain a high level of student access to computers; 98% of the nation's schools have Internet access (Cattagni & Farris Westat, 2001). Tools such as graphing calculators, Geometer's Sketchpad®, Excel spreadsheets, and PowerPoint® help math and science learners visualize and make connections (Heiser, 2004). Future educators must be able to master technological tools like these; student growth will be linked to teacher growth (Jacobs, 2001). Teachers of the future must be prepared to handle online learning, video conferencing, and even a paperless and wireless teaching and learning conference (ASCD, 2004b).

We are starting to see the effects of these kinds of shifts in educational focus. The U.S. Department of Education reported that fourth and eighth graders have made significant gains in mathematics on the National Assessment of Educational Progress:

> The percentage of fourth graders demonstrating at least a proficient level in math rose from 65% in 2000 to 77% in 2003—a 12-point jump.

> Among eighth graders, 68% scored at the basic level in math in 2003, up from 63% in 2000 and 61% in 1996. (National School Boards Association, 2003, p. 1)

Antonia Cortese, first vice president of the New York State United Teachers, attributed these gains to math instruction specialists, professional staff development, an improved curriculum aligned with state standards, and academic intervention (New York State United Teachers, 2003).

Creating math instruction specialists is beyond the scope of this resource, which does not attempt to teach mathematics and science to professionals who already have the knowledge base. The problem of teacher certification in mathematics and science stems from the fact that many states do not require elementary school teachers (who primarily teach in self-contained classrooms) to be certified in math and science. Upper-middle school and high school teachers who teach math and science as specialty subjects, on the other hand, are required to be state certified. At any level, however, teachers who are not certified in math and science cannot adequately prepare children in basic math and science requirements.

Ensuring Success in Math and Science: Curriculum and Teaching Strategies for At-Risk Youth further develops ideas from *Nurturing At-Risk Youth in Math and Science* (Tobias, 1992). This volume continues to address the plight of at-risk children who struggle to master mathematics and science, explores why American students fall behind in math and science as they progress through the higher grades, and offers proven curriculum and teaching strategies to address the complex issues that contribute to math and science failure.

Part 1 conceptualizes the problems behind failure in math and science, defines long-range goals, and describes the research and philosophy that support those goals. Closing the math and science performance gap will require the collaborative efforts of state departments of education, colleges and universities, and local school districts. It will require us to hold all students to high expectations and to revisit the way standardized tests are created, administered, and evaluated.

Part 2 discusses in detail how to redevelop math and science curricula to ensure success for all children. Collaboration is critical to curriculum redevelopment and effective education. Each school must work with school administrators, educators, and families to conduct its own needs assessment, and then design and implement a curriculum plan to address its students' needs in math and science.

Part 3 provides tested examples of math and science lessons that were developed in collaboration with teachers. Each lesson is followed by a brief analysis of its significance to meeting the challenges of ensuring success in math and science for at-risk learners. Also included are lessons that families and caregivers can use to reinforce math and science at home.

Strategies are concentrated in the elementary and middle grades (K–8) since proficiency in these subjects should begin as early as pre-kindergarten. Math and science skills are linked to the development of children's ability to read and critically think, which should also begin as early as pre-kindergarten. The *Multiplying Inequalities* study (Oakes, 1990) and the Third International Mathematics and Science Study (1995) both state that K–8 children (particularly children at risk) must be afforded the opportunity to take critical subjects in elementary and middle grades as preparation for math and science subjects in high school. Professional organizations such as the National Council of Teachers of Mathematics and the American Association for the Advancement of Science also support K–8 early intervention.

Although this resource was inspired by the plight of at-risk learners, the strategies presented here have profound implications for all American children and their future success as adults. Math and science skills are already crucial in the marketplace. To prepare our students for the *future* marketplace, in which math and science are sure to be even more vital, we must first prepare ourselves. Fortunately, we have the benefit of the math and science of educational research, which has shown that by using the right strategies, we can ensure success in math and science for all of our children.

Part 1

Fundamental Problems and Long-Range Strategies

Fundamental Problems Causing Math and Science Failure

■ ■

It is very important that educators understand the fundamental causes of math and science failure in America. Too often, theorists and practitioners address only the symptoms of problems and develop short-range, temporary solutions. Solving fundamental problems requires time, money, institutional collaboration, patience, and commitment. Meeting these types of challenges will yield permanent solutions that allow all children to succeed in math and science.

Fundamental causes of math and science failure among America children, particularly at-risk youth, are as follows:

- Insufficient pre-service preparation of teachers
- Insufficient professional development of teachers
- Homogeneous grouping and tracking of students
- Poor preparation of students for high school math and science

Insufficient Pre-Service Preparation of Teachers

Unfortunately, many teachers do not understand the actual content of math and science curricula well enough to teach these subjects. Math and science inadequacy are particularly profound among elementary and sixth-grade middle school teachers, who may not have had a concentration or a major in these areas. Elementary school teachers, in fact, are often expected to teach *every* subject in their self-contained classrooms. A study by the National Academy of Sciences found that "nearly 60 percent of eighth graders in American schools—double the international average—are taught math by teachers who neither majored in math nor studied it to pass a certification exam" (Herszenhorn, 2006a). Children will not learn math and science if teachers are inadequately prepared in the content. When "specialty" teachers in math and science are not available, math and science skill deficiency is the end result.

A related problem is that future teachers of math and science do not receive adequate training on how to *teach* math and science effectively. Pre-service teachers still receive:

- Little or no preparation on how to teach mathematics from a contextual perspective

- Little or no preparation in helping children develop the critical thinking skills needed to solve math and science problems

- Little or no preparation on how to apply math and science to the daily lives of children

Undergraduate education on how to teach math and science has improved, particularly since the National Council of Teachers of Mathematics and the American Association for the Advancement of Science released their guidelines for teacher education in 1989. But American undergraduate teaching methods still do not appear to measure up to those in other industrialized nations. This finding is corroborated by the 1995 Third International Mathematics and Science Study and an earlier study conducted by the Rand Corporation (Oakes, 1990).

Insufficient pre-service preparation of teachers affects at-risk children the most. These children need consistency, structure, and timely intervention to master math and science; teachers must be aware of those needs and prepared to meet them with proven strategies. Principals of racially mixed and high-minority schools often complain that teachers lack the interest and the preparation to teach, which causes serious problems for students and the school as a whole. In contrast, "[secondary] schools whose students are predominantly economically advantaged and White and suburban schools employ teachers who are, on average, more qualified" (Oakes, 1990, p. viii–ix).

Unfortunately, the students who are the most likely to need superior instruction are least likely to receive it. The fact that low-income and minority students have less contact with qualified math and science teachers indicates not only the low number of these teachers available, but also the large variation in certification status and in academic and teaching experiences. Conversely, middle-income and white students have greater access to math and science teachers who are certified to teach their subjects.

Insufficient Professional Development of Teachers

Insufficient pre-service preparation makes professional development for practicing teachers of math and science particularly critical, and yet in some cases the lack of pre-service preparation makes it difficult for professional development to be truly effective. Poor content preparation continues to be a major barrier to science and math teacher education, both before and during service.

In the current secondary education model for preparing math and science teachers, teachers take content courses from math and science departments, and methods courses from the education department. A pre-service teacher would be lucky to attend a course taught by a professor of science education or math education. This missing link between content knowledge and content-specific pedagogy must be connected, then, during a teacher's active service. Teachers of math and science should take a research approach to their teaching, using their experience to determine best practice, but they must also receive ongoing professional development from outside experts.

On the subject of mathematics, Manouchehri (1998) points out the following:

- Educational researchers have noted that many teachers lack a conceptual understanding of mathematics. In addition, substantial evidence indicates that teachers attending professional development sessions lack not only the necessary conceptual framework, but also the necessary basic math skills to understand and implement new knowledge.

- Mathematics preparation for teachers of middle and secondary levels occurs outside of teacher education. The subject matter for higher math is so complex that teachers can't expect to receive pre-service content instruction adequate to inform their teaching practice. It is therefore incumbent on the superintendent or district to provide supplementary, inservice instruction by bringing in experts for professional development. This of course is expensive and out of reach for schools with large populations of at-risk students and little funding.

On the subject of science, Eick, Ware, and Williams (2003) suggest that new science education teachers blame their university preparation, including disconnected coursework and inadequate field experiences, for their lack of professional preparation. Professional development could fill these gaps, and there are many national organizations that could provide this instruction. The National Science Foundation, the National Science Teachers Association, the American Association for the Advancement of Science, and many others provide standard materials, books, tracts, literature, and conferences.

Superintendents and principals sometimes argue that it is hard to find qualified math and science substitutes to allow these specialized teachers to attend conferences, but there are other alternatives. One teacher can attend and train others on return. Someone from outside the school can offer onsite professional development in best-practice teaching strategies for math and science; sometimes master teachers from elsewhere in the district can provide that service.

To make professional development effective, the school must have a principal who is an instructional leader, as Ron Edmonds and those in the Effective Schools movement have argued. To improve teacher education and student learning, the principal must be someone who can leave the office, see and understand what's happening in math and science classrooms, and support math and science teachers through a commitment to specialized professional development.

Homogeneous Grouping and Tracking of Students

Research conducted over a 30-year period concludes that children who are homogeneously grouped according to their ability do not learn as much as comparably skilled children in heterogeneous classes. In particular, children who have been isolated onto a remedial track have less access than other children to knowledge, powerful learning environments, and resources (Oakes, 1985, 1990; Oakes & Guiton, 1995; Rosenthal & Jacobson, 1968; Welner & Oakes, 1996).

The problem is not only that at-risk students who have been grouped and tracked into low-ability classes tend to be taught by teachers considerably less qualified than those teaching other classes (Oakes, 1985, 1990; Oakes & Guiton, 1995; Rosenthal & Jacobson, 1968; Welner & Oakes, 1996). There is also the problem of the "self-fulfilling prophecy" (Cooper, 1979; Good & Weinstein, 1986; Rotberg, 2001). Teachers communicate their varying perceptions and expectations of student performance through varying behavioral patterns; each student picks up a clear message of what the teacher expects. This message affects the student's self-concept, motivation, and performance. As time passes, these consistent teacher attitudes and instruction will mold the student's achievement level as well as social behavior (Brophy & Good, 1974). High expectations, for example, result in high student achievement. The converse is also true. A child on a "remedial" track will have a hard time getting off that track.

Heterogeneous grouping, by contrast, eliminates child labeling, the elitism of gifted classes, and the low academic expectations of children on "remedial" tracks.

Poor Preparation of Students for High School Math and Science

In an interview, Robert Moses, the pioneer advocate for equity in education, concluded:

> Too many poor children and children of color are denied access to upper-level math classes—to full citizenship, really— because they don't know algebra. . . . To participate fully in a world driven by computer technology, to be able to get a job that supports a family, you have to be literate in math—and that requires that you have to be at least literate in algebra by the time you go to high school. (Checkley, 2001, pp. 6–7)

This statement is also supported by the National Science Foundation's survey of 6,000 teachers among 1,200 schools. The study, *Multiplying Inequalities: The Effects of Race, Social Class, and Tracking on Opportunities to Learn Mathematics and Science* (Oakes, 1990), examined access to math and science education among various groups of students as indicated by five significant areas:

- The distribution of judgment about ability;

- Access to science and mathematics programs;

- Access to qualified teachers;

- Access to resources; and

- Access to classroom opportunities. (Oakes, 1990, pp. vi–x)

The study concluded, "With the exception of slightly greater amounts of time allocated to mathematics instruction in elementary schools with high concentrations of low-income and minority children, students from groups that as adults consistently achieve and participate less in science and mathematics have less access to science and mathematics curriculum" (Oakes, 1990, p. vii).

Even more alarming, this study pointed out that these students have fewer opportunities to take critical courses that prepare them for science and mathematics study beyond geometry. Even if the courses are available, at-risk students disproportionately fill low-track courses and so are otherwise excluded from these educational opportunities.

Other Problems

Other issues also affect children's potential to succeed in math and science. Standardized testing, gender inequities, and technology are three critical problems that are beyond the scope of this resource to resolve but worth discussing in brief.

Standardized Testing

When our children fail to reach the higher academic standards that we value so highly, we often blame the victims or the societal dynamics that create conditions for failure. We know, for example, that when an industry moves out of an urban center, a domino effect of unemployment and poverty can lead to low academic achievement.

We rarely focus our educational research on the assessment tools and state examination policies that hurt children and make them victims of test failure. Thousands of students across the nation are faced with the prospect of not receiving a standard diploma as a result of failing state exit exams (Ashford, 2003). Students, parent groups, and other organizations have launched protests and have filed lawsuits because of this phenomenon. California, Florida, Louisiana, Massachusetts, and New York are among the states that are either postponing or rethinking their exit examination policies.

Researchers must probe whether state standards are unrealistic. Educators must always help children reach their highest potential, rather than set an unachievable goal. This is done through quality teaching and realistic measurement; the highest potential may differ from child to child.

What about actual errors within state exams? Flaws in the New York State Regents Math A Exam, for example, led to an unusually high failure rate in 2003 (Errors Plague Test Makers, Educators, 2003). Errors are possible not only in the content of these tests, but in their administration and scoring. In fact, the increased use of standardized tests has resulted in a nationwide critical shortage of psychometricians, the trained experts who develop, administer, and score exams: "Many states lack officials trained to oversee testing and make effective use of score data" (Herszenhorn, 2006b).

In view of the academic standards and sanctions outlined in the No Child Left Behind Act (U.S. Department of Education, 2002), errors in tests—however minor—can have repercussions not just for students who are denied diplomas as a result, but also for schools who may fall behind national requirements. More focused educational research and concrete recommendations are needed on state examination polices as they relate to the success and failure of children.

Gender Inequity

It used to be held that boys were intrinsically better at math and science than girls. We now know that girls have just as much potential as boys to succeed in these subject areas, as long as they are not the victims of bias in teaching methods, teacher attitudes, instructional materials, or self-perception. Penny Hammrich, director of the Equity Studies Research Center (ESRC) has conducted and sponsored research to promote gender equity in science education. ESRC produces publications and educational programming dedicated to the advancement and education of women in science, technology, engineering, and mathematics. The center asserts:

> While legal barriers to achieving gender equity in American society have been removed, many barriers still stymie females. Research states that females hold "barriers of the mind" that prevent them from pursuing academic and professional careers in science, mathematics, technology, and engineering. (Hammrich, 2004)

These "barriers of the mind" are created by myths held and perpetuated by men—particularly those who have power and influence—that women neither have the aptitude nor propensity to succeed in math and science or to make contributions in these areas. In January, 2005, for example, Harvard University President Larry Summers presented a speech on gender disparities. Part of his theory in explaining the gender gap among top-tier tenured science professors was that men may have more "intrinsic aptitude" for high-level science (Ripley, 2005, p. 51).

Though the issue of gender equity in math and science has been discussed and researched for over 20 years, it is still a viable research issue, particularly in the areas of math and science equity for African-American and Latina women.

Other suggested areas of math and science equity research include how student gender affects the quality of education. How are male and female students treated differently when they pursue math and science as a career? How do the students themselves approach learning differently? What role do curriculum content and orientation and teacher attitudes and behavior play? We must understand that the perpetuation of the "barriers of the mind" myth begins early.

Technology

Finally, new findings and projections for both mathematics and technology will affect the future success of today's students. The research of Russell, BeBell, O'Dwyer, and O'Connor (2003) has discovered that despite substantial federal spending on computer-based technologies for students as well as teachers, there are questions concerning the extent to which technology is actually affecting teaching and learning. Expenditures, access, and use of computer-based technologies on the part of students and teachers increased significantly between 1995 and 2001: Federal dollars spent on educational technology increased from $21 million to $729 million, and the national student-to-computer ratio decreased from 9-to-1 to 4-to-1. A synopsis of their study concludes that although access to computer-based technology in schools and classrooms has increased, teachers use technology more for communication and class preparation than for actual instruction or learning activities that require student use of technology.

There is some "light at the end of the tunnel," however, as mathematics teachers across the country are beginning to employ interactive technology that provides instant information about student progress. One example of this procedure can be found in the Canton school district in Ohio. There, when a teacher writes out an algebraic function and asks students to find its value, students use calculators or "personal systems" such as the T-1 Navigator to electronically send answers to the teacher. Within seconds, an image appears on the screen in front of the class, indicating how many students selected the correct answer: "These systems enable teachers to gauge whether group of students or individuals have grasped a math concept" (Cavanaugh, 2006, p. 10).

Summary

The forerunners of the standards movement began in the 1970s when high school students exhibited compounded academic skill deficiencies, resulting in parental lawsuits of local school systems that granted high school diplomas to illiterate youth (Tobias, 1989). Pressure from the standards movement has led local school districts to increase their demands on teacher accountability and student performance—with positive results. In New York, higher standards were adopted by the state Board of Regents in 1996, and by 2001, more than 70% of all elementary schools met the new standards for mathematics (Sandberg, 2002). When the National Council of Teachers of Mathematics (NCTM) established new standards in 1989, math teachers in Columbia, South Carolina participated in a needs-assessment, and Columbia College developed new graduate math courses according to the results of the assessment to help middle school math teachers who lacked secondary math certification develop attitudes and strategies needed to adhere to the new standards (Snead, 1998).

In science, major professional science organizations such as the National Science Foundation, the National Science Teacher Association, the American Association for Advancement of Science, and the National Academy of Science are promoting standards for hands-on, inquiry-based science instruction that makes real-world connections. Educators should integrate instruction of the various science disciplines (such as biology, chemistry, and physics) as well as integrate science with other subject areas. Educators are listening. Elementary and middle school classrooms found in Springfield, Oregon; Concord, New Hampshire; Whitman Massachusetts; Wilmington, Delaware, and other cities across the United States are already engaging their students in these new strategies to give students opportunities to apply science knowledge and to make connections between what they learn in school and their everyday lives (Willis, 1999).

American educators can meet the challenges of math and science failure. The following chapter presents concrete solutions for these long-range problems.

Long-Range Strategies

This chapter addresses how fundamental problems that cause math and science failure among American children, particularly the educationally at-risk, can be resolved. Even though the resolution of these problems is long-ranged, the problems must be tackled simultaneously with short-ranged approaches if meaningful change is to take place.

Problem One: Insufficient Pre-Service Preparation

The deliberations of the National Council of Teachers of Mathematics and the American Association for Advancement in Science suggest that pre-service math and science teachers must learn contemporary teaching methods that are consistent with the ways in which they will be expected to teach. The recommended teaching methods will allow students to:

Mathematics	Science
• Apply mathematics to real-world settings.	• Apply specific scientific conceptual principles that pertain to the living environment.
• Learn mathematics through the integrated study of other subjects.	
• Use mathematical analysis to pose questions, seek answers, and develop solutions.	• Recognize the historical development of ideas in science.
	• Use scientific analysis to pose questions, seek answers, and develop solutions.
• Understand relationships and common themes that connect mathematics, science, and technology.	• Understand the relationship and common themes that connect science, mathematics, and technology. (National Research Council, 1993)
• Communicate and reason mathematically. (National Council of Teachers of Mathematics, 1989)	

Providing prospective math and science teachers with the best teaching methods and practices requires a collaborative effort between the institutions that influence pre-service teaching methods and practices:

- State departments of education

- Colleges and universities

- Local school districts

State Departments of Education

Since the 1970s, pressure from parents, community organizations, industry, and professional educational associations have influenced a wave of state educational reforms in response to poor student academic performance. In order for these reforms to be truly effective, however, state departments of education must work with teacher education programs to ensure that new teachers understand the reforms and develop their curricula and teaching strategies accordingly.

Whereas state departments of education traditionally developed curriculum *guidelines,* they now establish more precise *standards.* These standards must be incorporated into the pre-service phase of teacher preparation. Lesson plan aims should be aligned with state standards (see part 3, pages 89–164, for examples), and prospective teachers must learn strategies for accomplishing those aims.

State departments of education are also responsible for developing standardized tests that measure and assess children's academic proficiency levels in meeting state standards. Prospective teachers must be aware not only of how these assessments are designed, but also of how they are administered and scored. They should be taught how to incorporate this knowledge into their curriculum as part of their annual planning.

State departments of education approve teacher education programs and certify their graduates. As a result of the standards movement, the approval (and re-approval) process has become more rigorous. The documents that teacher education programs submit to the state usually include:

- Mission and vision statements

- Broad goals and specific objectives

- Activities designed to meet the stated goals and objectives, along with timelines

- Internal and external resources that would enhance the program's ability to realize its mission

- Total amount of courses offered and credits, along with course designations (program requirements or electives) and categories (foundation courses, major courses, or field courses)

Deans, directors, and department chairs of teacher education programs must take advantage of this natural collaboration with state departments of education to obtain the latest information about curriculum standards and assessment procedures, and tailor their programs accordingly.

Strategy: Rubrics

Rubrics are one way to help pre-service teachers align their strategies with state standards. An instructional rubric describes varying levels of performance for a specific learning task and simultaneously provides sequential direction. Some state standardized tests have employed rubrics to assess children's critical thinking skills. Despite a controversy that suggests rubric-based assessments produce data that are neither valid nor reliable (Berger, 2003), prospective teachers should be taught how to develop and use rubrics in the classroom. Regardless of their value for accurate *assessment,* rubrics still appear to be good *teaching* strategies. Instructional rubrics:

- Make teachers' expectations clear.

- Support the development of academic skills.

- Provide children with more informative feedback about their strengths and areas in need of improvement as compared with other forms of classroom assessment.

- Enable children to engage in self-evaluation.

The last two points are particularly helpful for new teachers and at-risk students. An instructional rubric describes varying levels of quality of performance for a specific learning task in explicit terms. Both student and teacher can use the rubric to evaluate whether the student has achieved success and to learn what must yet be learned to demonstrate mastery. Table 2.1 shows an example of an instructional rubric for fifth-grade science.

Colleges and Universities

Research findings of college and university faculty can be utilized to strengthen the teaching methods of pre-service teachers. The research of Barrett (1992), Hollander (1977, 1990), and Wilson (2002), for example, would enhance math and science teaching skills.

Strategy: Contextual Learning

The power of contextual learning is one teaching strategy that has emerged from such research. Everard Barrett, a former professor of mathematics education at the College of Old Westbury, State University of New York, and Sheila Hollander, a former professor of reading at Adelphi University, have conducted extensive research on the role of language and literacy in the teaching of mathematics in particular.

Gradations of Quality			
4	**3**	**2**	**1**
Observe and Describe			
Describes shapes, colors, weights, and volumes of common objects.	Describes shapes, colors, and weights of common objects, but not volumes.	Describes only shapes and colors of common objects.	Gives vague descriptions; does not use specific points of reference.
Compare and Contrast			
Compares and contrasts observable properties of solids, liquids, and gases.	Compares and contrasts observable properties of only two elements.	Compares but cannot contrast observable properties of elements.	Gives vague comparative and/or contrasting descriptions.
Group			
Groups common articles based on two attributes (such as shape and texture). Explains classification scheme utilized.	Groups common articles based on two attributes, but unable to explain classification scheme utilized.	Groups common articles based on only one attribute. Unable to explain classification scheme utilized.	Gives vague explanations for groups of common articles.
Classify			
Uses scientific equipment to classify objects using length, weight, and volume. Explains the classification scheme utilized.	Uses scientific equipment to classify objects using only two properties. Uses colors to indicate a classification scheme.	Uses scientific equipment to classify objects using only one type of measurement. Unable to explain classification scheme utilized.	Unable to use scientific equipment to classify objects. Unable to explain the use of classification schemes in general.

Table 2.1: An Instructional Rubric on the Nature of Matter for Fifth-Grade Science (adapted from Florida Department of Education, 1993)

Barrett (1992) maintains that children understand the meaning of many words, phrases, and sentences that are neither found in a dictionary nor explained by parents, but rather understood by the way words and sentences are used. This process is called *contextual learning.* For example, if a parent were to say to a child, "I would be *remiss* if I did not warn you about the dangerous dog in our neighbor's yard," the contextual term in this sentence is "remiss." A child might not understand the word "remiss" on a vocabulary exam, but he or she would understand the general sense of it in this sentence. If he or she heard this word in context several times, the child would eventually realize that "remiss" must mean "careless" in carrying out a responsibility or duty. Mathematically, if a teacher were to say to a class, "*Compute* the value of N, if N + 4 = 7," the contextual term in this sentence is "compute." After hearing it used in this context several times, the class would eventually realize that "compute" must mean to solve a problem or equation by using a mathematical process or calculation. In both examples, children would not use a dictionary to determine or define meaning, but rather their own mental analyses and critical thinking skills, as engaged by the process of contextual learning. This kind of mental exercise is crucial for the intellectual development of at-risk children.

If children have the capacity to retain contextually related information, Barrett argues, the same cognitive process can be activated or transferred to facilitate the learning and retention of mathematics—particularly in at-risk students. The application of the contextual method yielded excellent results among children who attended public schools located in Atlanta, Boston, Nassau County, New York, and Brooklyn (Barrett, 1992).

Hollander's study highlighted significant communicative teaching skills:

Teachers should provide opportunity for regular discussions of the rationale behind the correct solutions of a problem. These discussions may be held either before a problem is attempted or subsequent to its completion. It is to be expected that all students, not just the individual reporting on his own rationale, should benefit from these explanations that serve to facilitate the student's organization of knowledge. It appeared that questioning encouraged the students in this study to reconsider their behaviors and to refer again to the test in order to supply answers. Therefore, the teacher might experiment with techniques requiring students to review the facts presented within a problem and the relationship of these facts to each other rather than merely to review the computations employed. Questioning and discussion appear to be basic and profitable techniques worthy of regular employment within the elementary classroom. A technique resulting in a 40% improvement in altered responses is worthy of additional investigation. (Hollander, 1977, p. 661)

Hollander's later work, *Oral Reading Accuracy and Ability to Solve Arithmetic Word Problems,* provides additional pre-teacher training guidelines in the use of whole language skills by employing specific teaching skills of rereading and/or rewording the problems in question. Hollander suggested that children should be provided opportunities to read the problem orally and provide their interpretation of the material (Hollander, 1990).

Strategy: Whole-Language Approach

Edward O. Wilson, a research professor and the honorary curator in entomology within the Museum of Comparative Zoology at Harvard University, proposes teaching science by using the power of storytelling. Wilson (2002) believes that adults and children alike live, learn, and relate to others through stories. He suggests that scientific topics such as energy, matter, the solar system, and mammals, if presented as stories, would engage children's emotions and imagination during the process of learning. This methodology is empirically supported by brain research, which maintains as a central tenet that the brain functions by constructing narratives (McGee & Wilson, 1984; Jensen, 1998).

The common thread that bridges the research of Barrett, Hollander, and Wilson is the use of a whole-language approach to teaching math and science. The whole-language approach integrates listening, reading, writing, vocabulary development, and oral expression: As children use these skills to develop a clearer understanding of the subject matter, they simultaneously develop critical thinking skills. Critical thinking, in turn, involves problem-solving, drawing inferences, finding main ideas, finding facts and details, and understanding cause-and-effect relationships. The use of whole language in the teaching of math and science will enhance critical thinking and therefore must be a critical component of pre-service teaching methodology.

Local School Districts

Collaborative models for upgrading the quality of pre-service as well as in-service education have been in existence for over 20 years. Meaningful collaboration between teacher education programs at colleges and local school districts builds quality relationships and ensures that pre-service teachers learn best practices. The restructuring of pre-service and in-service education in North Carolina, for example, was a result of a quality assurance collaboration between the University of North Carolina's Board of Governors and the state's Department of Education (Liaison Committee on the Quality Assurance Program, 1981).

Strategy: Early Field Exposure

Such collaboration can bring about early field exposures prior to traditional student-teacher training. During early field exposure, prospective math and science teachers:

- Have opportunities to compare and contrast excellent, fair, and poor math and science lessons.

- Develop an understanding of how learning in math and science takes place.

- Have time to decide—before it is too late—whether they have chosen the right profession. The student-teaching experience usually occurs toward the end of a pre-service teacher's course of study, *after* he or she has invested time and energy in the certification process. Earlier field exposure would help potential teachers understand their future career sooner.

Exploring educational theory within specific, real-world classroom settings provides more realistic experience and produces more meaningful learning than lectures or seminars by actively involving pre-service teachers in teaching (More, 2003; Wolf, Carey, & Mieras, 1996). More suggests that her study, combined with the research on student-teaching, pre-service teaching behavior, and constructivist theory, amounts to a paradigm shift with respect to the structure and focus of early field experiences:

> Perhaps the development of more field practica prior to student-teaching in which pre-service teachers, university faculty, and mentor teachers routinely reflect on and examine concrete classroom situations for opportunities to integrate theory with practice and vice versa would provide the vehicle for such a change. Such a structure could potentially provide support for the formation of a set of schematic relationships on pedagogical "Gestalts" (Korthagen & Kessels, 1999) for the pre-service teacher to carry into the student-teaching experi-ence and eventually, their own classrooms. (More, 2003, p. 41)

New York City Public School 499 provides a more recent example of how meaningful collaboration between teacher education programs and local school districts demonstrates best teaching practices to pre-service teachers, strengthens practices of in-service teachers, and ultimately results in children reaching their highest learning potential.

Public School 499 is a collaborative effort between the New York City Department of Education, and Queens College of the City University of New York. Known as the Queens College School for Math, Science, and Technology, PS 499 serves as the laboratory school for Queens College math and science education faculty to conduct research. PS 499 teachers also demonstrate best teaching practices to math and science pre-service teachers who attend Queens College. This collaboration began in September 2001.

During the 1998–1999 academic year, New York state and New York City adopted new assessments to measure students' achievements of new and higher standards in mathematics. During the spring term of 2000, the California Test for Basic Skills (CTB) Mathematics Test was administered to grades 3, 5, 6, and 7, and the New York State Mathematics Test was administered to grades 4 and 8. Considering that teachers were given less than a year to learn the new standards and retool their curriculum, the children from PS 499 performed remarkably well. The spring 2000 results showed that just over 42% were able to meet the new standards, and almost 53% showed partial achievement. Only 5.3% of the children fell below standard (New York City Public Schools, 2001–2002).

Public School 499 students also excelled on tests that measured their abilities outside the school's core areas of math, science, and technology. The results of the Language Arts section of the Early Childhood Literacy Assessment System (ECLAS), administered to children in K–3, were very high. During the 2002–2003 school year, many of these young children performed at fifth- and sixth-grade levels (New York City Public Schools, 2002).

The ECLAS examines four areas: phonemic awareness, phonics, reading and oral expression, and listening and writing. The test does not examine proficiency in math and science per se, but it does measure the language skills that are so essential to success in math and science. The early incorporation of whole language to enhance critical thinking is a must in the teaching of math and science—particularly for at-risk children. One study (Georgia Study, 2003) showed that early intervention at the pre-K level significantly improved children's pre-math, letter and word recognition, vocabulary, and oral expression. Though children from all backgrounds showed significant improvement, economically disadvantaged children made dramatic gains. All children also improved in understanding printed materials, comprehending stories, and mastering basic skills. The effects of early intervention are also evident in the city and state test results of PS 499 children in grades 3–8 who scored at level 4, exceeding the learning standards for mathematics and showing a superior understanding of key math ideas (New York City Public Schools, 2002).

A laboratory school is not the only way to create early field exposure, however. In teaching exchanges between schools and teacher training programs, experienced educators can bring their real-world knowledge to students, and faculty can bring their research-based knowledge to teachers in the classrooms. During the 2000–2001 academic year, for example, Deborah King, principal of the Springfield School Region 3, taught the best administrative practices to graduate students at Queens College, and the author taught the best curriculum and instructional practices to teachers at the elementary school. This collaborative model bridged theory with the best and most current practices and could be easily implemented with undergraduate and graduate pre-service teachers of math and science.

Problem Two: Insufficient Professional Development

Effective professional development for teachers should achieve two goals. First, professional development must provide teachers with research-based approaches for measuring and enhancing the development of children's critical skills. This kind of in-service preparation is particularly crucial for math and science teachers since standardized tests now emphasize the *process* of solving problems, rather than just the *result* of correct answers. Second, there is a need for a new form of professional development that encourages teachers to involve themselves in the development of new knowledge; teachers can serve as action researchers who assist in the creation of new solutions to learning problems of children (Darling-Hammond & McLaughlin, 1995; Lieberman, 1995; Sparks & Hirsch, 1997).

Six Strategies for a New Paradigm of Teaching and Learning

In 1991, the AT&T Foundation sponsored the development of models for improving the preparation of urban teachers through college and public school collaborations at five sites across the United States. These five experiences yielded six instructional strategies that are particularly germane to the preparation of math and science teachers:

1. Assess the learning needs and styles of elementary students, and adapt instructional delivery to meet those needs.

2. Integrate higher-order thinking skills into the daily curriculum.

3. Use cooperative and team learning as primary instructional delivery strategies.

4. Use instructional strategies that raise student perceptions of their abilities and potential.

5. Use various technologies in daily instructional activities.

6. Integrate subject area content into realistic contexts for urban students. (Fountain & Evans, 1994)

Strategy: Action Research

In brief, action research is an *applied form of inquiry* that uses scientific research methods in examining the cause and effect of a social problem or practical issue. Common characteristics of action research include:

- A collaboration between the researcher and the participants

- A constant interplay or action revolving around reflection and the collection of data

- The development of a plan of action that responds to the issue being researched

- The sharing of research results with the school, the school district, and the local school board (Creswell, 2002)

Action research procedures are quite detailed so as to keep and maintain objectivity. Teachers as action researchers must be trained to utilize the following procedures:

- Stating the problem to be addressed or researched

- Developing research questions that are germane to the problem. These questions surround issues of scope, major causal factors, and possible solutions.

- Using data collection methodology such as target population surveys, key informant surveys, and focus groups

- Presenting the data collected [quantitative (statistical) or qualitative (descriptive) evaluation]

- Summarizing the major findings (sharing interpretations and conclusions drawn from the compiled data)

Action research is effective because it:

- Gives teachers tools to discover answers to problems scientifically, rather than depending on opinions or educationally guessing.

- Provides teachers with a research approach for enhancing and measuring critical thinking development of children.

- Encourages teachers to involve themselves in the development of new knowledge that would assist in the creation of new approaches toward solving children's learning problems.

- Can repair holes found within teaching methods related to test preparation, testing conditions, grading, and proper ways of integrating technology (Creswell, 2002, p. 614)

As early as 1995, teachers at Sawyer Elementary School in Ames, Iowa used action research to understand students' problem-solving techniques in mathematics. They gathered data on how well students could restate mathematical problems and how adept children were at selecting strategies to solve problems. Action research also helped these teachers identify a need to sharpen their own questioning skills (Falvey, Givner, & Kimm, 1995).

At Bay Shore Middle School in New York, educators used action research to analyze why their students struggled on state exams. They learned that math vocabulary was a problem—not just for students, many of whom spoke English as a second language—but also for teachers. "We gasped the first time we saw a question that asked for a 'multiplicative inverse,' because most of us use the term 'reciprocal,'" one teacher said (Sandberg, 2002 pp. 12–13). In response, teachers developed vocabulary assessments and introduced vocabulary bingo to math class. As another teacher noted, "Yes, math is numbers but you still have to be able to communicate clearly" (Sandberg, 2002, pp. 12–13).

Strategy: Educational Leadership

Educational leadership is essential to student success in math and science. Principals must become instructional leaders within their schools and rally all teachers to embrace collaboration, inclusion, action research, and in particular the philosophy of high expectations. The belief that all students can learn is essential, particularly for students who are victims of child abuse, substance abuse, suicide, AIDS, homelessness, and other tragic circumstances. As chapter 1's discussion of the effects of homogenous grouping and tracking revealed, academic performance is influenced by the student's perception of what level of performance is expected—for better or for worse. High expectations are particularly important for at-risk children because of the psychological and emotional issues they bring to the classroom may lower their self-esteem.

Educational leadership at Bay Shore Middle School in New York was key to the remarkable results in midlevel math among eighth-grade students in 2002. In the face of state sanctions if test scores did not improve, the number of students passing the eighth-grade math test leapt from 44% to 74% in a single year (Sandberg, 2002). Bay Shore's students face considerable challenges outside of the classroom: One third of the student population receives free or reduced-price lunches. The principal, Steven Maloney, stated that the increase in math achievement "took an incredible amount of time and energy" (Sandberg, 2002, p. 13).

The concept of time and energy in this case can be translated into collaboration among the school's educational administration, teachers, parents, and a suppertime school board. This collaboration brought about effective planning, resources for academic intervention services, a commitment to math test item analysis, and quality professional development opportunities (Sandberg, 2002).

Deborah Wortham, principal of one of the worst-performing elementary schools in Baltimore, Maryland, rallied her teachers to create and maintain a culture of high expectations—not only for the school's at-risk student population (all of the students were on free or reduced meals), but also for the teachers themselves. Her collaboration with teachers began with benchmarking best teaching practices and applying those practices in the classroom. Even though Wortham was a new principal, her school was nationally recognized for significant improvements in student academic achievement—after only 1 year (Allen, 2004).

Teachers should undergo different types of professional development tailored to their level of experience, but even experienced teachers may benefit from reviewing some fundamentals of good teaching.

Problem Three: Homogenous Grouping and Tracking

The problems of homogenous grouping and tracking still permeate school culture despite more than 30 years of research that disavow the effectiveness of these practices. Creating a heterogeneous environment means developing an environment of equity, in which children are perceived as equal irrespective of ability, exceptionability, race, socioeconomic status, or gender.

Strategy: Inclusive Education

In response to the question, "What is an inclusive school?" one set of researchers quoted from Carl Sandburg's poem "Names": "There is only one child in the world and that child's name is All children" (as quoted in Falvey, Givner, & Kimm, 1995, p. 1). We have developed inclusive classrooms to provide educational delivery services for children with disabilities, and we can develop inclusive schools to provide educational equity for all children. Inclusive schools would mean that at-risk children would be full members in every classroom, and that curriculum and teaching, particularly in math and science, would accommodate their needs in terms of materials, resources, and qualified teachers:

> Inclusive education is about all, making a commitment to do whatever it takes to provide each student in the community and each citizen in a democracy an inalienable right to belong, not to be excluded. Inclusion assumes that living and learning together is a better way that benefits everyone, not just those who are labeled as having a difference (e.g., gifted, non–English proficient, or disability). (Falvey, Givner, & Kimm, 1995, p. 8)

The implications of inclusion education for at-risk children, particularly in the areas of math and science, are tremendous. A truly inclusive education would require measures that ensure every student chances for academic success. To create classroom environments that are conducive to learning for all children, the following measures would be necessary:

1. Elementary teachers would have to be certified in the math and science content areas.

2. Elementary teachers would have to employ best teaching practices to ensure that all children can meet state testing standards.

3. Elementary teachers would have to embrace the philosophy of high expectations for all children.

Problem 4: Poor Preparation for High School

One conclusion of the RAND study (Oakes, 1990) stated, "With the exception of slightly greater amounts of time allocated to mathematics in elementary schools with high concentration of low-income and minority children, students from groups that as adults consistently achieve less in science and mathematics have less access to science and mathematics curriculum" (p. viii). Children at risk struggle with math and science not because they are incapable of learning these subjects, but often because they are simply not offered the appropriate classes. By the time they reach high school, they are ill-prepared for higher level topics in these subjects.

Strategy: Correlates of Effective Schools

The challenge of preparing children at risk adequately for high school math and science goes far beyond teaching and learning. A larger perspective that embraces the entire elementary and middle school experience is needed, such as the Effective Schools movement developed by Ron Edmonds during the 1970s.

Several of the correlates of Effective Schools are essential to this whole-school effort to prepare children at risk for high-school math and science. *Principals as effective instructional leaders* must insist on the appropriate elementary and middle school curriculum, and develop *a vision that is shared by teachers and families,* so that children receive support at school and at home. This vision must include *high expectations* for all children—regardless of race, ethnicity, socioeconomic status, gender, or mental, emotional, or physical challenges—to inspire both teachers and students. *A safe, orderly and non-oppressive learning environment* is essential for children at risk. *Frequent monitoring* (assessment) of the teaching-learning process will yield early academic intervention strategies for children struggling to master content (Association for Supervision and Curriculum Development, 1991).

Once Effective Schools principles are firmly established and enforced, elementary and middle schools will be able to establish opportunities for children at risk to experience focused preparation for high school math and science.

Affording at-risk children opportunities to experience critical subjects as preparation for math and science in high school depends upon four processes:

1. Conceptualizing a K–8 math and science curricula that:

   • Introduces math and science concepts.

   • Presents problem-solving opportunities.

   • Uses interdisciplinary teaching.

   • Introduces math and science multicultural personalities.

   • Shows the role of math and science in every day life.

   • Presents fundamental math and science courses on grade level.

2. Organizing a K–8 math and science instructional program

3. Providing effective pre-service preparation for beginning teachers of math and science

4. Providing professional development opportunities for experienced teachers of math and science

Chapter 4 discusses in detail the process of reconceptualizing and organizing K–8 math and science curricula and programs. Professional development ideas for beginning and experienced teachers of math and science will be discussed in detail in chapter 5.

Summary

Insufficient pre-service preparation means that inexperienced teachers entering the workforce are not exposed to enough contemporary mathematics and science methods that are consistent with ways in which they are expected to teach. Significant exposure to the best teaching methods and practices depends upon the contributions of state departments of education, colleges and universities, and local school districts to the education and training of pre-service teachers:

Addressing the problem of insufficient in-service preparation depends upon the impact of new and improved professional development. Professional development must:

1. Provide teachers with proven approaches for measuring and enhancing children's development of critical thinking skills.

2. Encourage teachers to involve themselves in the development of new knowledge of and new approaches to children's learning obstacles.

Addressing the problem of homogeneous grouping and tracking requires developing a school environment of equity where all children are perceived the same way irrespective of ability, exceptionability, race, or gender. Developing inclusive schools appears to be the answer to the challenge of equity. In inclusive schools, at-risk children would be full members in every classroom, and curriculum and teaching, particularly in the areas of math and science, would accommodate their needs in terms of materials, resources, and qualified teachers.

Affording at-risk children opportunities to experience critical subjects since preparation for math and science in high school depends upon reconceptualizing K–8 math and science curricula and organizing these curricula into concrete instructional programs. School administrators must then offer professional development opportunities so best instructional practices are available to all teachers.

The next section turns to the short-range solutions that will address the fundamental problems of math and science failure on a classroom level, including curriculum redevelopment, curriculum design, and curriculum implementation.

Part 2

Short-Range Strategies

Curriculum Redevelopment

Curriculum development is a joint process between state boards of education and local school districts. State boards of education make formal recommendations and issue guidelines as to what the curriculum should contain and how it should be organized (Ornstein & Hunkins, 2004). Local school districts then assign curriculum specialists, teachers, and administrators to a committee to set macrolevel curriculum goals. Sometimes parents and students are included in this process.

Other participants influence curriculum development as well. Educational publishers, testing organizations, and professional organizations like the National Council of Teachers of Mathematics and the American Association for the Advancement of Science have had significant influence on math and science curriculum development and assessment (Ornstein & Hunkins, 2004).

But what works in a particular elementary or middle school may not work for other schools a few miles away within the same school district. It is crucial, therefore, that the process of curriculum redevelopment in math and science addresses particular academic needs within a given school. The four phases to the curriculum redevelopment process are:

- Building support for the mission

- Allocating resources

- Conducting a needs assessment

- Modifying the curriculum redevelopment mission

Building Support for the Mission

The first phase of curriculum redevelopment is developing a school environment that supports institutional change. If the school principal is an instructional leader with an overall school vision and a curriculum redevelopment mission, he or she must first convince the school community to embrace both. The school community would consist of the site-based management team, supervisors, teachers, noninstructional personnel, parents, and children. Curriculum redevelopment should be an ongoing goal of the school's long-range planning document. Convincing a school community to embrace an educational leader's vision and mission would require a separate treatise. Continuous redefining of curriculum to meet changing standards should be a given. The particular definition or vision for the current cycle of redevelopment will require support as well.

Mutual trust between the principal and his or her constituents is paramount. Trust of any leader evolves out of a constituency's sense of that leader's professionalism, judiciousness, patience, humility, and perseverance. A leader can't build support for his or her mission without trust.

Allocating Resources

When a school is finally primed for the redevelopment process, funding, time, human resources, and space must be available.

Funding

The funding of a curriculum redevelopment effort is important and can be quite complex. In fact, the process of securing monetary support is so intricate that an entire chapter could be devoted to the subject. From a broad perspective, there are approximately six sources of funding curriculum redevelopment endeavors.

1. Tax levy funds: Since fundamental support of public school operations such as teacher salaries, textbooks, building construction, and norm-referenced testing uses state and local tax dollars, proponents of curriculum redevelopment should first attempt to secure funding from tax levy sources. Educational tax levy sources vary from state to state and may include property tax, sales tax, and/or state income tax, for example.

2. Educational foundations: Educational foundations created specifically to assist a particular school district are a relatively new phenomenon. An independent community group in concert with one or two members of the school district community can collaborate to establish a not-for-profit corporation. This allows the district to write proposals for federal, state, and private funds; tap into school alumni for contributions; and sponsor a variety of fundraising endeavors.

3. Private funding sources: Industrial and family foundations can be huge funding sources, regardless of the size of the foundation itself. Some large urban municipalities have "foundation centers" that contain an abundance of foundation catalogues. Foundation centers can also be accessed online. Many local educational agencies also disseminate information throughout their local school districts about smaller private funding sources.

4. Fundraising: Parent groups or a combined school effort to raise funds can bring in additional funds needed to support curriculum redevelopment endeavors, such as additional text books, other reading materials, and software.

5. Community resources: Community agencies and local businesses offer a plethora of valuable goods and services that can be used to strengthen curriculum development efforts at no cost. Utility companies, for example, can strengthen a science energy unit by hosting a field trip or contributing guest speakers, printed materials, and software related to natural gas, oil, electricity, and solar energy. Computer companies may contribute hardware to bolster a school or classroom's technology program.

6. Government reimbursement: Finally, if funds have already been allocated to curriculum development without additional funding, a school or district may seek reimbursement for those expenses from the federal or state government. Monies allocated to curriculum redevelopment for at-risk children may be especially eligible for reimbursement.

Time

Time for curriculum redevelopment must be factored into the school's scheduling plan. Advanced yearly scheduling can create common preparation periods, monthly faculty meetings, weekend meetings, and meetings over the summer months that are designated for redevelopment and curriculum design. Once a school establishes redevelopment as an ongoing goal of the school's long-range planning document, it must allocate time to realize that goal.

Human Resources

Supervisors, faculty, and staff are all needed to do the actual "roll up our sleeves" work of needs assessment. Item analysis of test performance, textbook analysis, administration of key informant surveys, and focus-group studies must be performed via teams. Individuals on each team must be able to carry out their assigned tasks and record their progress. School supervisors such as assistant principals, directors, and administrative assistants can coordinate these team efforts; the group should include members from various levels of authority. Once teams establish their personnel and job descriptions, future meetings can focus on progress reports. This process will ensure that the objectives of the redevelopment process will be met in a timely fashion.

Space

A designated space within each school should be provided for meetings and for the accumulation, organization, and filing of materials and data.

Conducting a Needs Assessment

The second phase of the redevelopment process is to conduct a needs assessment. The areas to address are:

- Item analysis

- Textbook analysis

- Teacher observations

- Protocol materials development

- Key informant surveys

- Focus group development

Item Analysis

Since standardized tests are the measure of the success of curriculum, teaching, and learning, the first course of action in the needs-assessment process is to analyze items answered incorrectly and correctly on the math and science portion of standardized tests. Items answered incorrectly indicate areas in need of remediation, and items answered correctly indicate those needing enrichment. Enrichment is as important as intervention; after all, the fundamental mission of most schools is not to help children pass the minimum requirements, but rather to allow them to reach their maximum intellectual potential.

The Deer Park School District of New York, for example, used math, science, and language arts test-score analysis to make progress comparisons between assessments of students in grades 4, 8, and 11. Using these comparisons, the school district developed student profiles that indicated the intensity of academic intervention services needed to develop math and science proficiency (Organisciak et al., 2003). They designed specific academic interventions to improve math, science, and English language arts performance as a result of their test-score analyses. These interventions focused on test preparation, testing conditions, test grading, parent awareness and cooperation, student motivation, and the use of technology (Organisciak et al., 2003).

Persons having the skills to carry out item analyses can usually be found within the local school district, the educational testing agency, or a pool of educational consultants. These individuals might be a teacher or assistant superintendent in charge of curriculum.

Textbook Analysis

School textbooks and computer software must keep current with changing curriculum standards. Out-of-date or irrelevant materials and textbooks are a major problem for many schools and districts. Textbook analysis should be conducted at least every 3 years. It entails examining copyright dates, tables of contents, and topics and subtopics within book chapters to ensure that they are aligned with current standards.

Reys, Reys, and Chávez (2004) argue that until recently, most mathematics textbooks (third through ninth grades) were indistinguishable: Their tables of contents and units of instruction were nearly identical and relied on memorization rather than deep knowledge and an understanding of meaningful relationships. Textbooks for each grade level did not reflect the variety of state standards that exist.

In response to the low math performance of American children on national and international math assessments, the National Science Foundation developed an initiative to create math textbooks commensurate with curriculum standards and teaching strategies that reflect the National Council of Teachers of Mathematics' current research on learning. Reys, Reys, and Chávez (2004) point out that although the new textbooks still focus on core skills, they present the skills in relationship to the real world in which children live:

> At present, approximately 10–15% of U.S. classrooms use these "standards-based" textbooks. They differ from traditional mathematics textbooks in that they present mathematical ideas in various contexts and engage students in exploring ideas, solving problems, sharing strategies, and building new knowledge based on solid conceptual understanding. Teachers no longer simply "cover" material. Rather, they facilitate a classroom learning environment that encourages questioning, conjecturing, and problem formulation and values student thinking and multiple strategies. (Reys, Reys, & Chávez 2004, p. 65)

The deep knowledge and higher-order thinking skills that students develop as a result of these better textbooks will serve them well beyond the annual standardized tests.

Teacher Observations

Teacher observations are important to the needs-assessment process to determine not only teaching quality, but also teaching methodology: how teachers address areas of children's weaknesses in math and science (as determined by item analysis). Observations of experienced teachers are just as important as observations of novice teachers. Though the protocols surrounding observations are important—the pre-observation conference, the observation, and the post-observation conference—it may be necessary for supervisors to conduct "pop-in" visits to observe teachers who have significant skill deficiencies and to guard against the possibility of teachers substituting a special lesson that does not reflect their usual methods.

The pre-observation conference is critical because it prepares the teacher for the actual observation. The supervisor should discuss the purpose of the observation, the specific elements of the lesson that will be assessed, and how the teacher can use the results of the observation to improve his or her effectiveness. The teacher should also have an opportunity to raise questions.

During the observation, supervisors should study:

- The thoroughness of unit and lesson plans
- The teacher's ability to carry out basic teaching skills such as eliciting the lesson's aim from the students, using a motivational lead-in to the lesson, and reinforcing the main points of the lesson
- The teacher's ability to include all students in the lesson
- The teacher's questioning skills and ability to successfully answer student questions
- The teacher's classroom management skills

The post-observation conference presents an opportunity for the supervisor and teacher to share their impressions of the lesson's strengths as well as areas that need improvement. The supervisor should support the teacher's instruction by discussing:

- How to improve long- and short-range planning
- How to improve teaching skills and strategies
- How to improve children's ability to retain information
- How to assess children's learning behavior

A self-evaluation segment can make the teacher feel invested in the process; the supervisor should encourage two-way dialogue throughout the conference.

Teacher observations may reveal unqualified math and science teachers. These teachers may be retrained, or they may simply need to be replaced with qualified personnel. The feasibility of retraining teachers depends upon their willingness to be retrained. Most teachers are willing, and they do well during the retraining process. Unfortunately, there are those few who have entered the profession for the wrong reasons. Some do not have a love for children and the natural process of maturation; others have teaching skill deficiencies to such an extent that an in-service training cannot bring them to a level of minimum proficiency.

School administrators can assist teachers in acquiring the latest math and science information in the following ways:

- Devote at least four of the monthly principal/teacher conferences a year to the dissemination and discussion of math and science education trends.

- Encourage supervisors and/or teachers who are math and science proficient to work with other teachers to procure and use protocol materials. These conferences must be scheduled within the principal's long-range planner.

- Devote two professional development days to math and science skill development.

- Encourage teachers to consider taking graduate math and science education courses. Encouragement can be monetary if the local education agency offers tuition reimbursement or stipends. Sometimes special grants will be offered by federal, state, or municipal agencies. Nonmonetary encouragement can be offered in the form of a reduced teaching schedule or the placement of special written citations within teachers' personnel folders.

- Sponsor one or two teachers to attend a professional math or science conference; these teachers can then train other faculty on what they learned.

Developing Protocol Materials

What professional materials are teachers using to keep abreast of the latest math and science information? School administrators must encourage teachers to select their own professional literature and software, develop their own professional math and science goals and objectives, and then assist teachers by providing professional development opportunities.

Key Informant Surveys

Chapter 2 contains a brief discussion of in-service preparation emphasizing a form of professional development—action research—that encourages teachers to participate in the development of new knowledge about children's learning problems.

Key informant surveys are an action research method to collect needs-assessment data from teachers and noninstructional staff. The actual survey is in the form of a questionnaire designed to acquire data from individuals with firsthand knowledge of the problem being researched. If, for example, the problem under scrutiny is a group of students who are constantly late and have poor attendance, key informants would probably be the attendance officer, guidance personnel, and the school psychologist. This survey fulfills a very important requirement of quality research in that the responses can be considered reliable data since key informants are those specific personnel who have expert information. This instrument is administered by the teacher who is the action researcher.

The Lincoln University key informant survey model provides excellent guidelines for creating an effective written summary of the results. The report should include the following sections:

- Sampling procedures: Describe the criteria for selecting the key informants and specify the number surveyed.

- Instrumentation: Include a description of the instrument (questionnaire) used.

- Procedures: Describe procedures used to collect data, including how the respondents were contacted, how the instrument was administered to them, what the setting was, how the completed instruments were collected, and percentage of responses. Briefly discuss the data analysis procedures.

- Limitations of the method: Include limitations of the size of the key informant group, their representation of the range of interests, instrument reliability, and validity, procedures and implications of these limitations for your needs assessment. Constraints that affect the quality of data may be included. (Lincoln University, 2003–2004, p. 8)

Other research procedures that not only enhance the action research model but further enable the researcher to organize and analyze collected data should be included as well. These additional procedures are too numerous to discuss here but would be a suitable topic for professional development sessions.

Focus Groups

Schools can use focus groups, another action research method, to collect data from parents and children through interviews. This method of collecting data is acceptable if the researcher is employing qualitative analysis (the use of explanatory or nonstatistical treatment of collected data). If the researcher is going to employ quantitative or statistical analysis, however, he or she should administer a survey instead.

Typically, the researcher meets with a small group of participants (four to six individuals) to collect a shared understanding of the problem being researched. As in a key informant survey, the participants must represent a purposeful sample selection: That is, the participants should be relatively sophisticated about the problem being addressed. The combination of good interviewing techniques and a deep participant knowledge base will allow the researcher to facilitate a more indepth discussion about the problem.

An excellent focus group, for example, could be made up of students who are being asked to express their opinions about a few math or science textbooks that they are using. Useful questions that the researcher may ask might include:

- "What does your science textbook offer that you find most useful?"

- "Is your science book easy to understand? Please explain."

- "Describe some of the new ideas that you have learned from your science textbook."

- "Is your science textbook difficult to understand? Please explain."

- "If you could change your science textbook, what are some areas you would add? What areas would you drop?"

- "In what ways does your science textbook help you complete your homework?"

- "In what ways does your science textbook help you prepare for a test?"

Lincoln University recommends that reports on focus groups include the following components:

- Sampling procedures: Describe the members of each focus group. How many were there? How were they selected?

- Discussion questions: Include a description of the discussion questions and a rationale for each one, including its relationship to specific research questions.

- Procedures: Describe the procedures used to convene and conduct the group(s). Describe procedures used for recording the discussions and analyzing results.

- Limitations of the method: Include limitations of the sample(s), discussion questions, procedures, and implications of these limitations for the needs assessment results. Constraints that affect the quality of your data may be included. (Lincoln University, 2003–2004, p. 8)

The needs-assessment process takes time. Since most principals have to submit a 2- to 3-year long-range plan to the school district's superintendent, the needs-assessment process can be expressed as a goal along with a timeline for accomplishment. If, for example, the process is estimated at requiring 4 months of work, those 4 months could conceivably begin during the spring term and continue into the summer, given that time may be lost due to norm-referenced testing, graduation, and end-of-the-year administrative duties. Superintendents and principals can sometimes entice teachers to work during some weeks of the summer. Scheduled time for needs-assessment meetings within these 4 months can be created in the same ways as for in-service math and science preparation.

Modifying the Mission

The curriculum redevelopment mission should be modified based on the actual resources available, as determined by the needs-assessment teams, to reflect an achievable, realistic goal. The same school personnel who were involved in the redevelopment process should be involved in its modification. Modification in this respect may involve not only restating the mission, but also downsizing goals. The first group of goals may express the ideal, but the final set should be realistic, based on the actual resources and funds that are available.

Summary

This discussion presents the curriculum redevelopment process within a school in four phases:

1. Building support for redevelopment

2. Allocating resources

3. Conducting a needs assessment

4. Modifying the mission

Developing the proper school environment requires a shared common vision and mission, as well as allocating funding, time, human resources, and space. Conducting a needs assessment involves:

- Analyzing items answered incorrectly and correctly on math and science standardized tests

- Analyzing math and science textbooks by examining copyright dates, tables of contents, topics, and subtopics

- Observing experienced as well as novice teachers

- Developing protocol materials

- Conducting key informant surveys of teachers and noninstructional staff

- Conducting focus group sessions with parents and children

Once they have gathered all the materials and data, faculty and staff can modify the curriculum redevelopment goals based on the needs-assessment results and the actual support resources available in the school and design a course of action to improve problem areas.

The next chapter will address how to incorporate the results of the needs-assessment process into a curriculum design.

Curriculum Design

Once a school has assessed its needs and modified its curriculum mission to identify macrolevel goals, objectives, and activities, the design phase begins. The curriculum design team will need to conceptualize the curriculum; organize instructional programs; include scope, sequence, balance, and integration; and design curricula as subject-, learner-, or problem-centered. Finally, to ensure that all children master math and science, the curriculum design should take care to identify and meet the needs of at-risk learners.

In designing curriculum, it is important to remember the bigger picture. The needs assessment stemmed from a larger process—curriculum redevelopment. Curriculum redevelopment is a school activity generating from a larger curriculum development process that is the responsibility of state departments of instruction and local education agencies. Grade levels have been already established by these state and local agencies. These grade levels already contain bodies of knowledge that children are expected to master. Discussions about redevelopment, needs assessment, and curriculum design conceptualization are simply used to augment what has already been established by state and local educational agencies.

Conceptualizing the Curriculum

The first challenge is to conceptualize the curriculum based upon data accrued during the needs assessment. The variables to consider depend upon the needs of a given school. One school, for example, may need to conceptualize a curriculum for a single subject on a particular grade level. Another school may need to conceptualize a curriculum for more than one subject and more than one grade. If data from the needs assessment shows, for example, that science students need more opportunities to problem-solve, use practical applications, or perform laboratory operations, the curriculum design team should conceptualize a science curriculum that is problem-centered in its design.

The same school personnel who were involved with the needs-assessment process should conceptualize the curriculum, taking the following general steps:

- Examine the data carefully.

- Allow science or math specialty teachers led by a school supervisor to hold brainstorming sessions in order to formulate general curriculum guidelines.

- Present these guidelines to the entire faculty for their input.

- Consider hiring an educational consultant in math or science to aid in developing a finite curriculum concept that meets student needs and state and district standards.

This process of developing curriculum conceptualizations generates mental energy! It forces administrators to think about where to find funds and resources to support the wonderful ideas developed by the group. A curriculum concept can begin with an abstract idea and end with a concrete reality. A curriculum and teaching conceptualization drove Marva Collins, an outstanding American educator to transform a small class in her attic into a fantastic preparatory school on the west side of Chicago.

To conceptualize an effective K–8 math and science curricula, consider the following guidelines:

- Develop subjects that introduce math and science concepts and vocabulary using support materials including historical and present-day math and science multicultural personalities, concepts, and systems.

- Develop subjects at all grade levels that offer problem-solving opportunities, such as simple to complex puzzles, riddles, and word problems.

- Develop subjects that bridge math and science with everyday life. These subjects should offer both field and laboratory components.

- Revisit basic math subjects that cover sets, whole numbers, number theory, fractions, decimals, ratio, proportions, percent, integers, and rational and real numbers.

- Revisit subjects that introduce children to the world of higher math and science, such as algebra, geometry, physics, biochemistry, earth science, statistics, probability, measurement, and the use of technology in health and science.

Organizing Instructional Programs

The second challenge is to make the transition from a curriculum concept to a functional instructional program. Organizing an instructional program brings the design from an abstract idea to a concrete format.

The transitional work from a curriculum concept to a functional instructional program can be done by members of the original needs-assessment group or math and science specialty teachers, led by either a school or district supervisor of math or science or a specialty consultant. Some steps that will need to be taken include:

- Develop macrolevel math and science goals, objectives, activities, and formative and summative assessment strategies.

- Align goals and objectives with state and local standards.

- Select appropriate protocol, materials, and resources for teachers (such as professional textbooks, teacher guides, videos, and computer software in math and science). Resources include professional associations, agencies, guest speakers, and field sites in the areas of math and science.

- Obtain appropriate textbooks, videos, and computer software in math and science for children.

- Develop specific math and science pre–high school subjects for departmentalized classes. Develop microlevel goals, objectives, activities, and formative and summative assessment strategies for each subject.

- Develop math and science instructional strategies to strengthen critical thinking skills such as problem solving (see teaching strategies in chapter 5, page 77).

Including Scope, Sequence, Balance, and Integration

The third challenge in effective curriculum design is to ensure that the design includes scope, sequence, balance, and integration. Scope defines all of the subject/content that the curriculum will cover, sequence defines the logical order of topics, balance describes the appropriate weight given to each topic, and integration links the subject/content to other relevant knowledge and skills.

If data collected from an item analysis reveals that children are generally weak in understanding functions as graphs, for example, a school could begin by establishing a major topic. This topic could be expressed as: "To enable students to understand functions and their graphs." The *scope* of this topic would encompass information about functions, graphs (of linear, quadratic, and exponential functions, as well as of other common functions), and the coordinate system.

Sequence expresses the order in which subtopics should be presented. These sequential subtopics serve to break down the major goals of the design into individual tasks and describe what children need to know before progressing to the next task (see Figure 4.1).

An Example of Sequential Subtopics

Topic: To enable students to understand functions and their graphs.

Subtopic 1.   Enable students to understand the term "function."

Subtopic 2.   Enable students to understand graphs as they relate to functions.

Subtopic 3.   Enable students to understand the coordinate system.

Figure 4.1

The development of these subtopics within a unit plan, though specific to pupils within a given class, is similar to the more broad-based development of an overall curriculum (see chapter 5, page 75). Both involve stating objectives, creating activities, selecting materials and resources, and developing formative and summative evaluation strategies.

Balance expresses how much weight should be given to each subtopic. In the example topic of "To enable students to understand functions and their graphs," balance would ensure that students receive equal information on each subtopic of functions, graphs, and the coordinate system. Balance may be expressed in the curriculum by giving an approximate time to be spent per unit of instruction. Balance doesn't necessarily mean equal coverage of units of instruction in that a particular unit may need more time because the students may find a unit more difficult to comprehend. More time can be spent on more difficult topics, if other topics can be easily dispatched. In many situations the achievement of balance resides within the realm of teaching rather than design.

Integration directs teachers to connect various experiences and types of knowledge within the curriculum plan (Ornstein & Hunkins, 2004). The whole-language approach discussed in chapter 2 (page 29) is one form of integration. Inclusion of other subjects, such as music, art, and global studies, may also be part of integration. Interdisciplinary teaching and learning are essential to the development of children's critical thinking abilities.

Using the sample lesson in chapter 8 for grade 8 on determining the value of two unknowns by graphing an equation, curriculum integration could be expressed in the following ways:

- Whole language skills: Whole language skills will be developed through the introduction and explanation of new vocabulary terms related to the lesson's aim such as "graphing functions," "axis coordinates," "variables," "plotting," and "origin." Students will be also asked to orally express their interpretation of the lesson's aim.

- Inclusion of other subject matter: With respect to the subject of art, particularly drawing, "crosshatching" is directly relevant to the aim of the lesson. Crosshatching is a form of shading that combines two or more sets of parallel lines, one set crossing the other at an angle. Crosshatching is employed extensively in engraving and etching to produce tone through linear means. This technique and the language used to describe it ("parallel," "intersecting," and "angle," for example) closely resemble techniques and language used in mathematics (such as graph paper). In fact, "at one time, artists were taught to crosshatch their lines at a regulation 45 degree angle and in black ink only" (Simpson, 1987, p. 27).

- Historical math personalities and cultures: Dating back to approximately the beginning of the 30th century BC, the ancient Egyptians used a system of rectangular coordinate grids for their architectural planning. They used equally spaced vertical and horizontal lines similar to today's graph paper.

Designing Subject-, Learner-, or Problem-Centered Curricula

Finally, math and science curricula designs can be subject-, learner-, or problem-centered. Teachers can choose the best design to reach their students. A learner- or problem-centered design may be most effective with at-risk learners, who need to relate to the material personally and derive special benefit from developing problem-solving critical thinking skills.

Subject-Centered

A subject-centered approach makes the actual subject/content the focus of the teaching-learning experience. A subject-centered design would emphasize a mastery of the content via sound teaching and a multiplicity of other learning activities. This approach is most effective in upper middle and high school settings. Figure 4.2 (page 66) shows how a teacher can use a subject-centered design to identify learning outcomes and to select the strategies and resources that best support those outcomes.

Learner-Centered

The learner-centered approach establishes the learning needs of children as the center or focus of the curriculum. This approach adheres to the progressive philosophy of education and is most effective in elementary and early middle school settings. Learner-centered designs afford more opportunities for interdisciplinary strategies and team-teaching implementation. Macrolevel goals, activities, materials and resources, and formative and summative assessment strategies must also be developed. Figure 4.3 (page 66) shows how a teacher using this strategy might first establish the learner's needs, then create lessons that teach to those needs.

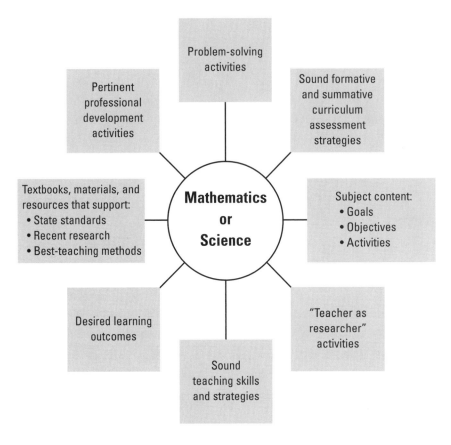

Figure 4.2: Subject-centered approach to curriculum design.

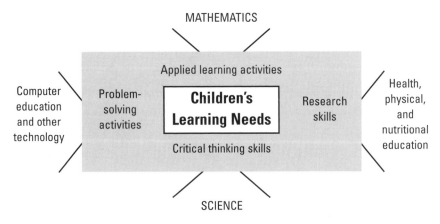

Figure 4.3: Learner-centered approach to curriculum design.

Problem-Centered

The problem-centered approach establishes situations, challenges, or problems of real living as themes of the curriculum design. Various subjects—such as math, science, and computer technology—are then related to the theme. This type of approach provides excellent opportunities to bridge theory with practice and show children the relationship of math and science to the real world in which they live. Problem-centered designs also afford opportunities for interdisciplinary strategies and team-teaching implementation. In Figure 4.4 (below), for example, the theme or problem is "Learning More About My Community." Various subjects such as mathematics, business, economics, and so on surround the theme. These subject areas make the experience integrative and therefore

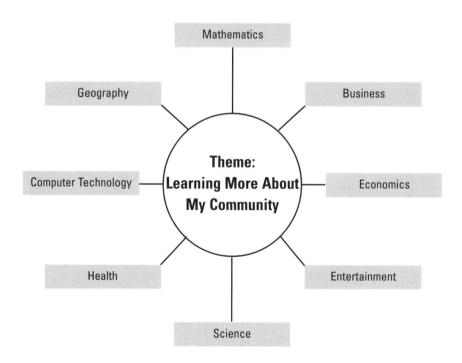

Figure 4.4: Problem-centered approach to curriculum design.

call for a team-teaching approach. This kind of design is particularly effective with at-risk children because it demonstrates the relationship of otherwise abstract subjects to their daily lives.

Designing to Ensure Success for At-Risk Students

All of these steps can be integrated into a learner-centered curriculum specifically designed to ensure that at-risk learners achieve mastery in math and science. The curriculum conceptualization should address the importance of higher thinking skills; subjects that offer problem-solving opportunities are particularly important. The curriculum should expose students to the world of higher math and science to prepare them for high school math and science curriculum (Moses & Cobb, 2001; Oakes, 1990). In particular, the instructional programs should include specific interventions for struggling students, and the design should be culturally inclusive in scope.

Interventions

Academic intervention strategies can be a significant facet of a learner-centered curriculum design. The following recommendations could serve as an academic and early intervention paradigm for at-risk learners:

- Educational counseling: One of the most essential elements of academic success, particularly in middle school, is educational counseling. At-risk students benefit not only from guidance on effective studying techniques and high school preparation, but also from assistance with personal problems that may interfere with academic success.

- Proactive tutoring: This approach assists at-risk students in the classroom during the lesson *before* there is evidence of academic difficulty, in contrast to typical reactive tutoring approaches. In the reactive model, students must first indicate that they are failing before help is assigned.

- Test-taking strategies: Many children, particularly those at risk, have anxiety when an examination is approaching. Teachers can help students explore studying and relaxing techniques that may improve their performance.

- After-school and summer compensatory programs: These programs are also effective early intervening strategies and should not be confused with remedial programs. Remedial programs are a reaction to failure, where as compensatory programs meet at-risk children's needs by offering tailored learning experiences including small group instruction, innovative teaching strategies, and special learning materials.

Connections

To reach proficiency in these subjects, at-risk children must understand the relationship between math and science and everyday life. When children realize that there's no mystery in math and science mastery, they lose their fear of the subject matter and become more open to learning. More importantly, at-risk learners will find it easier to apply math and science computations and concepts to daily practical problems than to abstract concepts. Two youngsters who discuss a short cut from their apartment building to the school yard will have more success in understanding that the shortest distance between two points is a straight line than two youngsters who only learn the abstract principle.

At-risk learners also benefit from making cultural connections to the subject matter. All students should be exposed to cultural diversity in the subject matter, but educationally at-risk minority students will receive extra benefit from understanding how their cultural groups made original contributions to the fields of mathematics and science. A culturally integrated curriculum gives children ownership in the knowledge base, builds cultural pride and positive self-image, and inspires children with confidence.

Multicultural approaches highlight the experiences of all cultures in the development of knowledge. Multicultural approaches do not discount Asiatic, European, African, or Native American approaches; rather, they challenge Eurocentric claims (overt or indirect) that Greece was the beginning of Western civilization (much less all civilizations). All ethnic groups have contributed to fundamental knowledge bases in philosophy, theology, logic, ethics, engineering, architecture, and mathematics and science.

If math and science subjects are taught from an interdisciplinary perspective, plenty of opportunities exist to introduce different cultures and personalities beyond the usual historical math and science personalities (Pythagoras, Marie Curie, Einstein, and so on). Consider, for example, the following figures in math and science:

- Ben Carson, M. D., neurosurgeon and director of pediatric neurosurgery at Johns Hopkins University Hospital in Baltimore, Maryland (African American): In 1987, Dr. Carson participated in the first successful separation of Siamese twins joined at the back of the head. It took 5 months to plan and 22 hours to actually execute the surgery, which involved a surgical procedure that Dr. Carson helped initiate. The social behavior and academic problems that Dr. Carson exhibited as a child in school would have probably labeled him as an at-risk youth today.

- Robert Moses, Ph.D. in mathematics (algebra) from Harvard University (African American): Dr. Moses initiated the Algebra Project, which uses math literacy and civil rights to develop a sense of empowerment in African-American children. He has launched his national math literacy program as a key to economic and civil equality.

- Srinivasa Ramnujan, 1897–1920, (Indian): Ramnujan, who emerged from a poor socioeconomic background in India, arrived at astounding results in number theory, without any formal academic training (Musser & Burger, 1994).

- Jaime Escalante, high school mathematics teacher, (Bolivian): At Garfield High School in East Los Angeles, California, Escalante helped low-income Spanish-speaking students perform so well on the Advanced Placement calculus exam that they were initially suspected of cheating (Musser & Burger, 1994). Escalante himself was suspended more than five times as a student; his mother introduced him to concepts like "sphere" and "circumference" by simply peeling an orange (Hanson & Graves, 2006).

- Masaru Ibuka (Japanese): Ibuka introduced the first pocket-sized transistor radio in 1952 (Trager, 1979). He improved the technology of transistor production by cutting the original 95% reject rate to 2% and reduced the cost from $6.00 to a fraction of $1.00 (Collins & Tamarkin, 1982; Carson & Murphey, 1990). The company he cofounded grew into the giant now known as Sony.

There are many other possibilities, of course. Teachers should create inclusive presentations that help students feel personally connected to the material.

Summary

This chapter discusses four challenges of designing effective math and science curriculum for K–8 students:

- **Conceptualizing a curriculum based on needs-assessment data**: This requires engaging children's whole language and problem-solving skills, bridging math and science classroom knowledge with children's everyday experiences, and introducing historical and present-day math and science concepts, systems, and multicultural groups and personalities. Fundamental math subjects must be revisited to reinforce children's operational skills, and higher math and science subjects must be introduced to prepare children for high school.

- **Organizing an instructional program**: Making the transition from a curriculum idea to a functional instructional program brings a design from an abstract idea to a concrete format. This format involves the development of macrolevel goals, activities, and formative and summative assessment strategies, along with appropriate protocol and student materials and resources. Goals and objectives must be also aligned with state and local standards.

- **Including scope, sequence, balance, and integration**: These elements ensure that students are taught the right content in a logical order, with appropriate emphasis to each area, and with connections to other relevant knowledge they may already have.

- **Choosing an approach**: Curriculum design can be subject-, learner-, or problem-centered. Choosing the right approach for the grade and skill level of the students will help ensure their success.

Educators can take specific steps to design a curriculum that will be effective for at-risk students by including academic interventions and making the subject culturally and personally relevant.

The next chapter will examine how a well-designed curriculum can be implemented through sound instruction and supported by targeted professional development sessions.

Curriculum Implementation

■ ■

Curriculum implementation represents the final stage of a long journey toward ensuring success in math and science for at-risk learners. Effective implementation requires sound instructional practice and relevant professional development.

Sound Instructional Practice

Much has been written on the teaching-learning dialectic. Research on learning styles, multiple intelligences, the emotional quotient, and the brain has revealed new information about how children learn, and new ways of teaching have been developed in response. New information resulting from dedicated research will always be relevant. However, for at-risk populations, the challenge of doing well in math and science demands early intervention, consistency, and a structured learning environment.

For over 60 years the research on cognitive and educational psychologists has laid the foundation for the value of early intervention. Jerome Bruner published his *Process of Education,* which represented the findings of the famous 1959 Woods Hole conference, in 1960. Jean Piaget began to publish his epistemological findings in 1964, and in 1965, the federal Economic Opportunity Act created pre-kindergarten programs called Head Start across the United States to assist young children from low socioeconomic backgrounds to develop their intellectual prowess; their middle-income counterparts already had the "home" advantage of books, games, traveling opportunities, and family discussions.

Early intervention is important, as Piaget's research shows that language and logico-mathematical thought begin in the second stage of child development (age 2 to 7) and continue through adolescence (Piaget, 1967). Russia's launching of the Sputnik satellite in 1957 caused Jerome Bruner of Harvard University to convene the famous 1959 Woods Hole conference of esteemed professors of math, science, psychology, education, and other important disciplines. In this conference, these scholars wanted to examine how American education in science might be improved in primary and secondary schools (Bruner, 1960). Improvement in science education on the primary level showed a definite emphasis on early intervention.

Consistency and a structured learning environment are also important for at-risk learners. These are created through sound instructional practice. Key elements of sound instructional practice include:

- Long-range thematic planning

- Teaching skills and strategies

- Supporting materials and resources

- Effective classroom management

- Appropriate assessment measures

Long-Range Thematic Planning

In long-range thematic planning, teachers establish a unit plan of instruction to cover 3 to 6 weeks. They develop goals that are driven by a unifying theme and aligned with state and district curriculum standards. Each goal is broken down into objectives, and each objective is further broken down into activities. The unit plan describes which formative assessments will be used as students complete the activities for a given objective, as well as what kind of summative assessments will be used at the end of the unit as a whole. Materials and resources are specified as well (see Appendix A, page 173, for a sample science unit plan).

Elements of a Unit Plan

Theme
Materials and resources
Standard(s)
Goals
   • Objectives per goal
   • Activities per objective
Formative evaluations (administered after each completed set of activities)
Summative evaluation (administered at the end of the unit)

In the next phase of long-range thematic planning, teachers use the unit plan to develop precise short-range lesson plans that meet the objectives of each goal. Each objective becomes a lesson aim.

Elements of a Lesson Plan

Daily lesson plans should be constructed using long-range thematic unit plans and should be structured to meet unit objectives (see sample math and science lesson plans in part 3, beginning on page 89). A lesson plan should specify:
   • State and/or district curriculum standard(s)
   • Aim
   • Skills taught
   • Motivational lead-in
   • Materials and resources
   • Procedures
   • Key questions (optional)
   • Reinforcement
   • Homework (optional)

Elementary and middle school teachers should develop math and science lessons into 3– to 6–week thematic units for self-contained classes. Specific math and science pre–high school subjects, such as elementary algebra, earth science, and elementary statistics, can also be developed for departmentalized classes.

Establishing themes opens opportunities for interdisciplinary lessons and, as a result, team-teaching presentations. Teachers can simultaneously ascertain the availability of needed school resources as they create long-range goals and objectives. Various teaching strategies can be utilized, such as problem-solving approaches, cooperative learning groups, and class reviews.

Teaching Skills and Strategies

All teachers should possess effective teaching skills and strategies. Teaching *skills* are discrete facets of teaching competence that all teachers should possess regardless of grade level or teaching specialty. Such skills include knowledge of the subject/content area and its central techniques of investigation. Teachers of math and science should be masters of their content area and adept in the arts of questioning and summarizing. Other significant teaching skills include the ability to select appropriate materials and resources (discussed in greater detail on page 78), to develop quality homework assignments including family-assisted lessons (see chapter 9), and to assess academic progress (see page 79).

Teaching *strategies* are made up of a combination of teaching skills and are designed to accomplish particular student goals and objectives. Teaching strategies include, for example, using cooperative learning groups, science research teams, culminating math and science activities, and contextual methods of teaching mathematics (see Barrett, 1992).

The Problem-Solving Approach

A problem-solving approach is especially helpful in teaching math and science as it stimulates the development of critical thinking skills that are foundational to math and science. This approach has three components: whole-group instruction to lay the conceptual groundwork of the unit, small-group cooperative learning to allow children to explore the material, and whole-group reviews to integrate the conclusions of the smaller groups into a collaborative solution. This combination of activities, while more complex for the teacher to implement than simple whole-class instruction, results in a creative, engaging learning environment for students.

1. **Whole-group instruction.** Activities within this sequence introduce procedures, materials, and language that children need for tasks they will pursue within the second sequence. Teachers can also use the whole-group instruction sequence to discuss the four phases of problem-solving: understanding the problem, devising a plan, carrying out the plan, and looking back (Swanson & Swenson, 1991). The first phase of problem-solving, understanding the problem, can then be accomplished as a whole-group activity.

2. **Small-group cooperative learning.** The cooperative learning sequence places children in smaller, heterogeneous groups to use math and science procedures, materials, and language learned in the whole-group sequence. Within these groups, children can execute the next two phases of problem-solving: devising a plan and carrying out the plan. Each small group engages in specific activities that lead to the solution of the problem. The likelihood of these phases being accomplished is quite probable, since cooperative learning contains the elements of positive interdependence, individual accountability, and collaboration.

3. **Whole-group reviews.** The final sequence of the problem-solving approach is whole-group reviews. Teachers can use this "looking back" phase to summarize and interpret results from each

group. This allows children to share their own thoughts and ideas about math or science relationships while making connections to the other ideas and concepts discussed.

Selection of Appropriate Supporting Materials and Resources

The selection of appropriate supporting materials and resources—books, magazines, educational games, software, guest speakers, and field trips—is one of the most important aspects of sound instructional practice in math and science. Innovative teachers can create their own materials. Finding or creating the right materials can enhance the professional growth of teachers as well as the educational growth of children.

Science becomes alive and more interesting when children are engaged in completing projects, making a functional apparatus, or going on field expeditions. These activities enhance learning far more than reading books or viewing a computer program. Expeditionary learning, for example, has developed in many urban schools in America, including Boston; New York; Portland, Maine; and Denver. Hawkins and Vinton (1973) emphasize that the environment outside of the classroom is a far more exciting place to learn than any particular school and a far more exciting teacher than any individual.

Effective Classroom Management

A teacher must create a classroom environment that supports teaching and learning. Developing such a classroom environment calls for mastery of specific aspects of classroom management: planning, self-management, classroom organization and design, and pupil discipline. Mastery of these would create an ideal learning environment for at-risk learners.

With respect to long-range *planning,* classroom organization, design, and children's routines must be thoroughly considered. Unit planning allows teachers to ensure in advance that the school has the resources and materials to support weekly lesson plans and daily activities. The teacher can then create daily routines that integrate into the long-term plan. When children know what to expect and what to do when they arrive in class—such as "copy the assignment from the board," or "open your notebook and read quietly,"—the teacher can spend less time on behavior management and more time on teaching. Planning and routine provide the infrastructure for learning.

The teacher's *self-management* is a matter of personal character. For example, is the teacher punctual and organized? Does the teacher understand exactly how to proceed from the point of arrival to the point of dismissal? If the teacher is not disciplined and displays an aura of confusion, as opposed to self-management, children will instinctively understand and exhibit poor behavior. *Classroom Management for Elementary Teachers* (Evertson, Emmer, Clements, & Worsham, 1997) is one helpful classroom management resource for teachers.

Classroom organization and design—how the teacher arranges classroom furniture and utilizes available space—can greatly influence the effectiveness of a learning environment. Creating room stations and using bulletin boards to display educational charts, pictures, and children's work will create an atmosphere of meaningful teaching, learning, and even excitement.

These three factors, combined with an insistence on maintaining children's routines, will result in a fourth factor crucial to classroom management—*pupil discipline.*

Accurate Pupil Assessment

Assessment of math and science skills, particularly with respect to at-risk children, should be criterion-referenced. Criterion-referenced assessment measures the mastery of specific objectives.

This process is also developmental, in that once children demonstrate proficiency in one objective, they proceed to the next level and a new objective. New objectives are extensions of preceding ones. The assessment of learning math and science from a criterion-referenced perspective renders immediate information about how much or how little has been learned. If formative assessment data indicate difficulty in learning a particular objective, the objective can be taught again using different methods and materials.

Criterion-referenced assessment builds confidence in children at risk because the assessment process does not result in achievement labels; students are measured by their progress on the subject matter. Norm-referenced assessment, by contrast, measures students against state, regional, or national norms, and places the student in categories or percentiles that may label them as slow, average, above average, or excellent. Children who fall into the lowest percentile are often looked down upon by the media, school, teachers, other parents, and even peer groups, and are grouped and tracked into low-achievement classes where subject matter can be watered down.

As earlier chapters have shown, negative labels and low ex-pectations contribute to low self-esteem and reinforce poor per-formance. The purpose of criterion-referenced assessment is to enable children to achieve mastery of a particular subject. If proficiency is not demonstrated after the first test, reteaching and using new materials will enable children to feel good about themselves as they learn. This process does not condemn the child for not knowing, but tells the child that he or she has a right to question and a right to struggle. The test results do not communicate, "You are a failure." Rather, the results tell the child, "You need improvement, and you and I will work together until progress is made."

Chapter 2 (page 23) discusses the use of instructional rubrics as one way of providing children with more immediate, criterion-referenced feedback about their strengths and areas in need of improvement in math and science. In addition, questioning children on how they arrived at solutions to arithmetic problems enhances their understanding of math and science procedures and will improve their test scores on the inevitable norm-referenced tests.

Professional Development

Beginning and experienced teachers of math and science need effective in-service preparation to teach math and science successfully. Professional development can use the results of the needs-assessment and curriculum redevelopment processes to target specific areas in which teachers may need to learn new methods and strategies. While even experienced teachers would probably benefit from a review of teaching basics and sound instructional practice, all teachers receive the greatest benefit from professional development that is geared toward their individual needs and levels of experience.

Beginning Teachers of Math and Science

New teachers benefit from:

- Site orientation
- Technological training
- Teaching protocol, materials, and resource guidance
- Pedagogical skills and strategies training
- Rubric development
- Long-range planning assistance

Of these, skills and strategies training, rubric development, and long-range planning assistance are the most crucial.

Site orientation should make new teachers familiar with the school's existing resources and protocol. Teachers should learn not only the location of materials, supplies, and software that are pertinent to the teaching of math and science, but also the requisition procedures for these resources if they are not immediately available.

Technological training should ensure that new teachers have mastered software that may be helpful to their teaching, such as PowerPoint, and should show new teachers how to maximize their use of computer and science laboratories and equipment.

Teaching protocol materials and resource guidance are specific forms of information that assist in the professional growth of teachers. They can be obtained in graduate courses or at professional development seminars and conferences. Professional educational organizations such as the National Science Teachers Association, the Association for Supervision and Curriculum Development, the National Council for Teachers of Mathematics, and the Council for Exceptional Children provide these materials for the professional growth of their constituents.

Pedagogical skills and strategies training are available through subject supervisors, master teachers, professional development consultants and district office personnel.

Rubric development, as discussed in chapter 2 (page 23), helps ensure that new teachers understand national, state, and school curriculum standards as well as the varying levels of proficiency that students may exhibit. New teachers should receive training on how to develop their own rubrics.

Long-range planning assistance to new teachers should stress the use of themes, interdisciplinary approaches, and aligning state and district standards with weekly topics and daily lesson aims.

Experienced Teachers of Math and Science

Experienced teachers will generally benefit more from opportunities to learn more about:

- Interdisciplinary approaches and cooperative group learning
- Curriculum mapping
- Action research

Interdisciplinary approaches heighten global thinking skills by showing the relationships between different subject matters, enabling learners at risk to understand that mathematics and science are a part of everyday living like art, music, language arts, and social studies. Heidi Hayes Jacobs and her colleagues began to introduce interdisciplinary teaching as a professional development concept in the early 1990s (Jacobs, 1989).

Cooperative learning first emerged at the turn of the 20th century, when John Dewey encouraged teachers to allow students to investigate and solve problems together in small groups (Ellis & Whalen, 1990). The concept is different from typical small-group instruction, however. Cooperative learning also stresses relationships. This teaching strategy is particularly important in math and science because it encourages children to share ideas and compare findings— much as scientists and mathematicians do in real life. Cooperative learning fosters positive interdependence, face-to-face interaction, self-assessment, constructive feedback, and discussion.

Interdisciplinary teaching approaches within cooperative learning environments are helpful to experienced teachers because many were taught to approach math and science as separate subjects, using a whole-group teaching strategy. Cooperative learning as a teaching strategy is a relatively new idea in teacher education courses, and teachers who have been working since before the 1990s probably did not learn about cooperative learning in their teacher training programs.

Curriculum mapping uses a database to collect and compare information on what teachers are actually teaching through the course of a school year. All teachers enter data about their curricula: its content, specific skills taught, and assessments used. Content might be entered as key concepts and essential questions; assessment can include tests, products, or performances.

Once all the information has been entered, teachers and administrators review the resulting "maps" to detect curricula differences within a particular grade level. They can identify areas for grade standardization, align their assessments with state and district standards, and consider ways to upgrade teaching strategies and materials to be more effective. The process of reviewing and refining curriculum maps should be continuous (Jacobs, 1997, 2001).

Curriculum mapping allows teachers to fine-tune the content of their classes to ensure that students receive consistent instruction across the grades and that the subject/content of each grade prepares students for the next. It can reveal significant gaps and overlaps. In a school with five third-grade teachers, for example, most people might assume that a single third-grade math and science curriculum is taught in all classes. Curriculum mapping may reveal, however, that there are actually five different curricula being taught. This can have serious consequences for students who are all taking the same norm-referenced tests; some may be better prepared than others through no fault of their own.

Professional development in *action research* shows teachers how to conduct research on learning problems in math and science—the precise learning problems exhibited in their own classrooms. As a result, teachers become originators of new knowledge tailored to their needs, rather than dispensers of old knowledge that may or may not be appropriate to the children they serve. Promoting action research can serve as the first step toward creating an overall school culture of inquiry.

Summary

This chapter presents sound instructional practice and professional development as two crucial aspects of successful implementation of math and science curriculum.

Sound instructional practice includes long-range thematic planning, teaching skills and strategies, selection of appropriate supporting materials and resources, effective classroom management, and accurate pupil assessment. Long-range thematic planning allows teachers to build 3- to 6-week units of instruction around a theme that is aligned with state and district curriculum standards. Teaching skills and strategies ensure that teachers have the required subject/content knowledge and can design activities to accomplish particular student goals and objectives. Selecting materials and resources to support their instruction is a separate skill, like assessment, that teachers must master. The specific aspects of classroom management include planning, self-management, classroom organization and design, and pupil discipline. Math and science assessment of at-risk children within the classroom should be based on a criterion-referenced, developmental approach.

Professional development should be provided for beginning as well as experienced teachers. Out of all the professional development ideas suggested for beginning teachers, teaching skills and strategies, rubric development, and long-range planning are the most critical. Experienced teachers benefit from training in curriculum mapping, action research, and special teaching strategies like interdisciplinary teaching and cooperative group learning.

The following section integrates the short-term strategies discussed in this section into fun, effective math and science lessons and activities for grades K–8.

Part 3

Creative Teaching and Home Reinforcement

Math and Science Lesson Plans That Work: Early Education

Daily lesson plans, as discussed in chapter 5, should be developed from long-range monthly units. Planning guides the teacher on a course of developing true learners. A lesson plan alerts children, supervisors, and even parents to a deliberate, organized course of action that will guarantee learning. Early childhood (pre-K–3) is perhaps the most important period within public schools because mental development during this time is crucial. Encouraging oral expression and introducing new vocabulary are essential steps in developing critical thinking. Bloom (1964) established that children develop 40% of their mature intelligence from conception to age 4 and another 30% from ages 4 to 8. These data indicate that from kindergarten (age 5) through third grade (age 8), children develop 70% of their mature intelligence.

Chapters 6, 7, and 8 provide sample lesson plans for math and science at various grade levels. These plans are flexible guidelines; they are not intended to provide a step-by-step prescription for success. A well-planned lesson allows for innovation but keeps teachers on a steady course toward accomplishing the lesson's aim. Teachers can incorporate their own strategies and teaching style into any of them.

The following elements must be included in a lesson plan that stimulates intellectual development of learners at risk:

- **State and/or district curriculum standard(s):** The state standard(s) should be posted in the classroom and referred to in the lesson plan so that supervisors and parents will see that the lesson is an attempt to meet specific criteria.

- **Aim:** Students should understand the lesson's goal: what they will be learning for the day. It is possible to elicit the aim from children using a skillful, motivational lead-in to the lesson. In every lesson, the aim must be aligned with state and local math and science standards. Once students learn those standards, they begin to understand math and science concepts, apply math and science principles to everyday situations, and can perform successfully on the norm-referenced tests that play such a large role in their futures.

- **Skills taught:** The lesson plan should clearly define subject/content and critical thinking skills that are necessary for a child's intellectual development. (During the early childhood years, tactile, manipulative, and social skills are also crucial, but this text will not delve into these multifaceted areas.) The integration of whole language, critical thinking, and technological skills throughout all lessons is crucial to ensuring success. Math and science cannot be taught in a vacuum, and children must experience and understand these interrelationships through vocabulary development, problem-solving, and using calculators and computers.

- **Motivational lead-in:** Motivational lead-ins are creative introductions to lessons designed to inspire students and spark their interest in a forthcoming lesson. A skilled teacher avoids saying, "Today, we are going to learn . . . " With practice, a teacher can actually elicit the daily aim from the children, through questioning, activities, video or computer presentations, or a simple narrative introduction.

- **Materials and resources**: This includes all the items students will use to enhance the learning process, such as books, magazines, charts, hardware, software, games, learning kits, and so on, as well as any special materials needed, such as paints, rulers, and so on.

- **Procedures**: Learning can be defined as the extent to which information imparted by the teacher is retained by the students and applied to problem-solving challenges. The math and science teaching procedures outlined in these chapters are crucial to helping at-risk students master the content.

All lesson procedures use the problem-solving approach discussed in chapter 5 (page 77). This approach involves three steps. First, in whole-group instruction, the teacher introduces and familiarizes students with the lesson, its terms and vocabulary, and the materials and resources they will use. Second, in small-group instruction, teachers can shift from talking "at" children in a lecture to talking "with" them—and facilitate their interaction to discover new facts and problem-solve together. This is a wonderful experience for both teachers and students. Instructional groups can vary in size. In the primary grades, children work well in pairs; by grade 4, children may benefit from working in threes. Advanced middle school students will be able to work in larger groups. The epitome of the small group experience is cooperative learning groups (see page 77). Finally, the third step of the problem-solving approach is review in the whole-group instructional mode. This gives students an opportunity to ask questions and teachers an opportunity to pose questions to test what each group has learned.

Procedures should always involve children in the fulfillment of the lesson's aim. Examples of other lesson procedures include interactive computer strategies, field trips, and general review sessions.

- **Key questions (optional):** Key questions can be incorporated throughout the procedures and may or may not be specified explicitly in the lesson plan. The best kinds of questions to pose to children are open-ended questions. These questions are formulated to elicit full-sentence responses rather than simple "yes" or "no" answers. Questions serve to review and probe the main ideas of the lesson, drawing out children who are not participating. Good questioning skills can also alert the teacher to the overall effectiveness of the lesson.

- **Reinforcement:** Reinforcement activities enable children to retain the main ideas of a lesson. There are essentially four types of reinforcement activities:
  1. The medial summary
  2. The final summary
  3. Homework
  4. Review questions to segue from the last lesson into a new lesson

- **Homework (optional):** Homework can reinforce the lesson taught that day or prepare students for the next day's new lesson.

Sample Mathematics Lesson Plan, Kindergarten

STATE STANDARD

Students will understand mathematics by applying mathematics in real-world settings.

AIM

To learn about taking inventory.

SKILLS TAUGHT

Whole-language skills: Students will develop vocabulary ("add," "sum," "total," "minus," "take away," and "difference"). They will practice writing, reading, listening, and oral expression.

Critical thinking skills: Students will practice counting in general and counting within specific categories. They will grasp the concepts of "inventory," "sequence," and "category." They will learn that there is more than one way to express a number. They will practice identifying shapes and comparing sizes.

MOTIVATIONAL LEAD-IN

Students will identify items that are the same and items that are not the same.

MATERIALS

Calendar, craft sticks, markers, charts, brown paper bags, crayons, buttons, plastic dinosaurs, and toy bears

PROCEDURES

Whole-group instruction: Discuss with students the meaning of the terms "inventory," "sequence," "category," "add," "sum," "total," "minus," "take away," and "difference."

- Students will count the amount of items that are the same.

- Students will count the amount of items that are different.

- Students will categorize items that are different.

- Students will learn different ways to express a number.

Small-group instruction (partners): Give each set of partners various amounts of different items such as plastic dinosaurs, toy bears, crayons, and buttons.

Each set of partners will arrive at different totals.

Each set of partners must use different methods to express their totals. For example, one set may count unlike items first, then like items, before adding the groups together. Another may count all items first, then separate (subtract) unlike items from like items.

REINFORCEMENT

Direct each set of partners to share their information with the other sets of partners.

Ask the students to express what they have learned today. Fill in any vital information that students leave out of their summary.

HOMEWORK

Ask the students to take an inventory of any small kitchen item at home, such as potholders, wooden spoons, or coffee cups. Give each student a written note that explains the assignment to parents and caregivers.

Activity Sheet
Comparing Shapes and Sizes

1. Compare the stars. Which one is small? Which one is large?

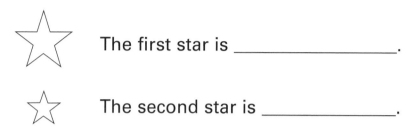

The first star is _____.

The second star is _____.

2. Arrange the circles in order from the smallest to the largest by writing 1, 2, 3, 4, or 5 inside the circles. Use 1 for the smallest circle and 5 for the largest.

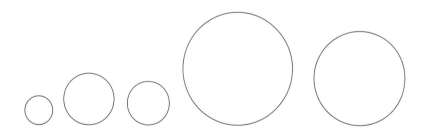

3. Draw a line between the squares that are the same size.

4. Circle the rectangle that can fit inside the circle.

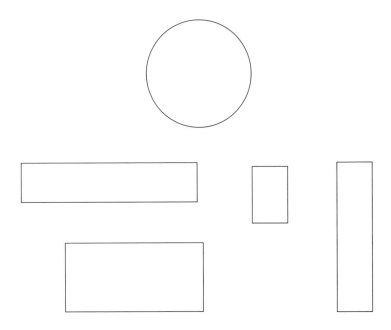

Activity Sheet
Counting

Use the pictures to make your own problems.
Count the shapes and write down your answers.

1.

_____ + _____ = _____

2.

_____ + _____ = _____

3.

_____ + _____ = _____

4.

_____ + _____ = _____

5

_____ + _____ = _____

4. I know that _____ + _____ = 6

_____ + _____ = 6

_____ + _____ = 6

Sample Science Lesson Plan, Kindergarten

STATE STANDARD

Students will understand and apply scientific concepts, principles, and theories pertaining to the physical setting and living environment, and will recognize the historical development of ideas in science.

AIM

To learn about trees and what they give to people.

SKILLS TAUGHT

Whole-language skills: Students will develop vocabulary ("trunk," "branches," "maple syrup," "sugar maple," "silver maple," "elm," "black oak," "white oak," "red oak," "turkey oak," and "sycamore"), learn how to pronounce consonants and consonant blends, and practice listening and oral expression.

Critical thinking skills: Students will practice problem-solving.

Science skills: Students will learn the different parts of a tree and what certain trees give to people.

Mathematical skills: Students will practice counting.

MOTIVATIONAL LEAD-IN

Place a bottle of maple syrup on the desk, and engage the students in a discussion about the many uses of maple syrup. Ask the students where they think maple syrup comes from.

MATERIALS AND RESOURCES

Tree jigsaw puzzles, charts of different trees, a center cut of an actual tree trunk, a book about trees, cards with pictures of tree shapes to recognize and match, tree leaves

PROCEDURES

Whole-group instruction: Ask students to count the rings on the center cut of the tree trunk. Explain how the number of rings shows the tree's approximate age.

Have students approach the tree charts and tag the various parts of the tree with the appropriate labels.

Read aloud a story about a tree, such as *The Giving Tree* by Shel Silverstein or the poem "Trees" by Joyce Kilmer.

Small-group instruction (partners): Give partners different procedures such as putting together a tree jigsaw puzzle, matching tree cards, identifying trees via tree leaves, identifying different parts of a tree via tree charts, or identifying trees by products. Facilitate instruction by going to each small group to ask and answer questions.

KEY QUESTIONS

"Can anyone name a tree by the shape and look of a leaf? How?"

"What new names have we learned?"

REINFORCEMENT

Ask the students to discuss some of the important facts that they learned about trees. Fill in any pertinent information that they omit.

Plan a field trip so that the students will be able to observe varieties of trees.

HOMEWORK

Instruct students to ask their families to help them name three things in their homes that are made from trees.

Sample Mathematics Lesson Plan, Grade 1

STATE STANDARD

Students will understand mathematics and become mathematically confident through the integrated study of geometry.

AIM

To learn about different geometric shapes.

SKILLS TAUGHT

Whole-language skills: Students will develop vocabulary ("right triangle," "pentagon," "hexagon," "octagon," "remainder"), practice oral and silent reading, and discuss shapes.

Critical thinking skills: Students will practice problem-solving and "scaffolding" (building on a prior knowledge base to determine what the next step is in a sequential learning process). They will demonstrate understanding of the concept of sequence.

Mathematical skills: Students will draw geometric shapes and will practice counting, adding, subtracting, establishing the remainder, and double-checking answers.

MOTIVATIONAL LEAD-IN

Display different objects, and ask the children to discuss the shape of each object.

MATERIALS

Coins, tiles, boxes, stencils of different geometrical shapes, pattern blocks, computers and software, clocks, MathStart® book series (HarperCollins), *Emeka's Gift* (Onyefulu, 1995), Junior Scholastic Reading Series

PROCEDURES

Small-group instruction (3 students per group): Ask students to create different geometrical shapes by using stencils of pre-drawn geometrical patterns such as rhombi, hexagons, and trapezoids.

Then direct students to take pattern blocks to fit against their drawn geometrical shapes (pattern blocks are small, wooden geometrical pieces in different colors).

Finally, ask students to count the amount of pattern block pieces used to create a geometrical shape.

Whole-group instruction: Ask students to discuss shape patterns that they created and wrote about.

REINFORCEMENT

Facilitate each group by asking the students to summarize their activities in sequential steps.

HOMEWORK

Direct students to take their shape patterns and arrange them into a design of their choosing. Use their designs in a class project, such as a "quilt" made from glued paper versions of their designs.

Activity Sheet
Understanding Sequences

1. Draw the two figures that should come next in the sequence.

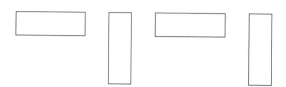

2. Draw the next five figures in the sequence.

3. Draw the next three figures in the sequence.

4. Redraw the following 10 geometric shapes in order of the number of straight lines each shape contains. Start with the shape with the smallest number of lines and end with the shape with the largest number of lines.

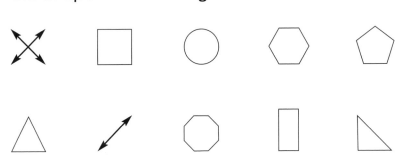

---

5. Name two shapes from question 4 that have the same number of lines:

The _____ and the _____

both have _____ lines.

The _____ and the _____

both have _____ lines.

6. Describe the difference between two of the shapes that have the same number of lines.

_____

_____

_____

7. Fill in the missing shapes:

In our classroom, both the board and the

door are shaped like a _____. The

clock is in the shape of a _____.

8. Name 10 things in your home that have at least 3 different shapes.

_____

_____

_____

_____

_____

_____

_____

_____

Sample Science Lesson Plan, Grade 1

STATE STANDARD

Students will understand and apply scientific concepts, principles, and theories pertaining to the physical setting and living environment, and will recognize the historical development of ideas in science.

AIM

To learn about whales and why they are important.

SKILLS TAUGHT

Whole-language skills: Students will read aloud and develop vocabulary ("whales," "mammals," "fish," "harpoon").

Critical thinking skills: Students will respond to open-ended questions in complete sentences.

Science skills: Students will learn about ocean zones, the composition of the earth, the fish food-chain, kinds of whales, the anatomical breakdown of whales, and characteristics of mammals and fish.

MOTIVATIONAL LEAD-IN

Ask the students to name some very large animals who live in the sea. Ask where and how they have learned about sea creatures.

MATERIALS AND RESOURCES

A large wall chart of the four ocean zones where different species of whales live, *Weekly Readers®*, a poster depicting a whale, and a taped whale song

PROCEDURES

Whole-group instruction: Identify some different kinds of whales, such as toothed whales, baleen whales, right whales, humpback whales, orca whales, white whales, and blue whales. Discuss why whales were hunted and the laws that were passed for their protection.

Small-group instruction (3 students per group): Give each group whale photographs and anatomical pictures of whales.

Ask each group to identify the types of whales displayed in the picture and to name the different parts of a whale. Direct students to describe the different activities of whales.

KEY QUESTIONS

"Why are whales mammals?"

"What other information can you share about whales?"

REINFORCEMENT

Review important concepts discussed during the previous lesson, such as the ocean zones and vocabulary words.

HOMEWORK

Distribute handouts depicting fish and whales and their characteristics. Ask students to indicate two differences between fish and whales on the handouts.

Sample Mathematics Lesson Plan, Grade 2

STATE STANDARD

Students will use mathematical analysis and engineering designs to pose questions, seek answers, and develop solutions.

AIM

To learn about symmetry.

SKILLS TAUGHT

Whole-language skills: Students will develop vocabulary ("symmetrical," "asymmetrical," "diagonal," "vertical," "horizontal," "hovering," "wedge," "pulley," "axle," and "lever").

Critical thinking skills: Students will apply reason to solve problems.

Mathematical skills: Students will learn the difference between symmetrical and asymmetrical shapes.

MOTIVATIONAL LEAD-IN

Place a kite assembly kit on a table. Ask two students to assist in assembling the kite. Discuss the assembled kite with the whole class in terms of its equal parts, geometric shape, and aesthetic qualities.

MATERIALS AND RESOURCES

Let's Fly a Kite (Miller, 2000), kite kit, math cards depicting symmetrical and asymmetrical shapes

PROCEDURES

Whole-group instruction: Read *Let's Fly a Kite* aloud to the class.

Small-group instruction (partners): Give each set of partners some math cards depicting symmetrical and asymmetrical shapes. Instruct partners to discuss the cards and decide whether the depicted shapes are symmetrical or asymmetrical.

REINFORCEMENT

Ask each set of partners to come to the front of the class, identify the shapes as symmetrical or asymmetrical, and explain the reasoning behind their decisions.

HOMEWORK

Instruct students to ask their parents to assist them in drawing two symmetrical shapes and two asymmetrical shapes.

Sample Integrated Mathematics and Science Lesson Plan, Grade 3

STATE STANDARD

Students will use mathematical analysis to develop solutions. Students will understand the relationships and common themes that connect mathematics and science.

AIM

To learn about capacity, using liters as units of measurement.

SKILLS TAUGHT

Whole-language skills: Students will write and develop vocabulary ("estimation," "liter," "volume," "capacity," "difference," "substitution," "cubic centimeters," "metric system," and "customary system").

Critical thinking skills: Students will practice problem-solving and reasoning.

Mathematical skills: Students will practice measuring, estimating, and rounding numbers to the nearest tenth and to the nearest hundredth.

Science skills: Students will learn the chemical makeup of water, how it is written in a formula (H_2O—2 parts hydrogen and 1 part oxygen) and how it is visually depicted using three circles, and the water density and importance of rain forests.

MOTIVATIONAL LEAD-IN

Bring out 1-liter and 1-quart containers. Ask two volunteers to fill each container to capacity. Then pose the problem statement: "How much liquid can a large container hold when it is full?"

MATERIALS AND RESOURCES

Small tubs of water, measuring cups, measuring syringes, computers, and software (Newbridge Discovery Links®)

PROCEDURES

Whole-group instruction: Engage the class in a general discussion about the different units of measurement using the metric and customary systems, such as liters versus quarts or kilometers versus miles. Ask the students to discuss the many uses of water.

Small-group instruction (3–4 students): Break the students into teams. Direct each team to scoop water out of a small tub with a measuring cup and pour the water into containers until each container is full (keeping track of how much water each container holds).

Then instruct students to remove some water from the containers with a syringe (the syringe must have measuring lines on it). Students can calculate the amount of water left by subtracting the amount withdrawn by syringe from each container, using the mathematical computation of subtraction.

Have each team record their results on "teacher made" forms.

REINFORCEMENT

Ask one student from each team to present and explain the team's findings.

HOMEWORK

Ask students to write down the following problem and answer it at home later:

If Frisky the Horse needs 10 gallons of water a day, how many gallons of water does Frisky need in a week? How many gallons does Frisky need in a month?

Alert students that they will be asked to discuss the mathematical processes they used to find the answer.

Direct students to also write a personal reflection of the day's lesson in their notebooks, encouraging them to use their new vocabulary words.

Activity Sheet
Understanding Systems of Measuring Liquids

Customary Measures	Metric Measures
1 quart = 32 ounces	1 liter = 33.8 ounces
1 pint = 16 ounces	2 liters = 67.6 ounces
1 cup = 8 ounces	3 liters = 101.4 ounces

Circle or fill in the correct answer.

1. A quart is (more or less) than a liter.

2. Two liters is (more or less) than a pint.

3. Two pints is the same as 1 _____.

4. A liter is (more or less) than 2 pints.

5. Three liters is (more or less) than 1 cup.

6. A quart is 32 ounces; 32 is between 30 and 40. Therefore, 32 is closer to (30 or 40).

7. A pint is 16 ounces; 16 is between 10 and 20. Therefore, 16 is closer to (10 or 20).

8. A cup is 8 ounces; 8 is between 0 and 10. Therefore, 8 is closer to (0 or 10).

9. The milk container we receive in the cafeteria is closest to (a quart, a pint, a liter, 2 liters, or 3 liters).

10. The liquid in a can of soda is 12 ounces; 12 is between 10 and 20. 12 is closer to (10 or 20).

11. The liquid in 3 12-ounce cans of soda is closer to (1 quart or 1 liter).

12. _____ is between 300 and 400. It is closer to 400.

13. You can pour 1 liter of soda into a 1-quart bottle (true or false).

14. You can pour 3 quarts of milk into a 3-liter pail (true or false).

15. You can pour 2 quarts of water into a 2-liter bottle (true or false).

16. If 2 quarts = 64 ounces, how many additional ounces are needed to fill a 2-liter bottle? (4.5, 6, 3.6, or 10)

17. If 3 liters = 101.4 ounces, how many quarts would come closest to filling a 3-liter bottle? (1 quart, 3 quarts, 2 quarts, or 4 quarts)

18. Jamal can pour a gallon (4 quarts) of paint into a can that holds (4 liters, 1 liter, 2 liters, or 3 liters).

19. The car that Mr. Lopez drives from home to his office uses 9 liters of gasoline. Mr. Lopez would need (9, 5, 45, 36) liters of gasoline if he drives to his office 5 days a week.

Answers

1. less

2. more

3. quart

4. more

5. more

6. 30

7. 20

8. 10

9. a pint

10. 10

11. 1 liter

12. Varying answers possible.

13. false

14. true

15. true

16. 3.6 ounces

17. 3 quarts

18. 4 liters

19. 45

Math and Science Lesson Plans That Work: Elementary School

■ ■

The early education lessons of the last chapter were built on the premise that children develop knowledge of the world around them through active involvement. Piaget's constructivist point of view holds that lessons must give children opportunities to develop their knowledge and ideas through their interaction with objects and other children; teachers should provide learning in activities such as the use of manipulative materials, cooperative work, open-ended questions with discussion, and the introductory use of calculators and computers. Each child builds his or her physical and logico-mathematical knowledge through their own action on objects (Kamii & DeVries, 1978).

The sample lessons in chapter 6 also introduced beginning math and science terms and concepts such as inventory, shapes, sizes, plants, animals, symmetry, and metric versus customary systems. Understanding these aspects of math and science at the early childhood level builds readiness for computation and problem-solving in the elementary grades.

Grade 4, which usually represents the beginning of the elementary grades, is crucial as the transitional grade from early childhood. For children at risk, fourth grade can bring a drastic decline in reading comprehension and critical thinking abilities if they have not been immersed in constructive-readiness teaching methods during their early childhood years. Hart and Todd (2003) suggest that by age 3, children from privileged families have heard 30 million more words than children from poor families. The researchers also suggest that this gap becomes wider and wider as children become older and are promoted to higher grades.

The lessons in this chapter show elementary school children how to apply their math and science knowledge and ideas through comprehension, critical thinking, and problem solving by way of computational skills. Probability, statistics, physics, equations, and graphing functions are some of the concepts that students from grades 4 through 8 are expected to learn. Teachers are expected to employ student involvement individually and in groups. Lesson plans should challenge students to use higher critical thinking in an effort to expose and apply computational skills to solve practical problems, analyze, and even conjecture. Lessons should also challenge students to use appropriate technology for computation and exploration. As the sample exercises provided here progress from grades 4 to 8, they gradually become more complex.

Sample Mathematics Lesson Plan, Grade 4

STATE STANDARD

Students will understand mathematics and become mathematically confident by communicating a reasoning concluded mathematically, by applying mathematics in real world settings, and by solving problems through probability.

AIM

To learn about probability.

SKILLS TAUGHT

Whole-language skills: Students will develop vocabulary ("probability," "event," "experiment," and "outcome"), discuss, and use complete sentences in response to open-ended questions.

Critical thinking skills: Students will conduct probability experiments and analyze their results.

Mathematical skills: Students will set up and solve an equation. They will express elements of the equation as an equivalent decimal or percent.

MOTIVATIONAL LEAD-IN

Produce a coin, state the mathematical problem to be solved— "What is the probability of the coin landing tails up?"—and ask a volunteer from the class to flip the coin.

MATERIALS

Pencils, paper, and coins

PROCEDURES

Whole-group instruction: Discuss the definition of "probability": the possibility that an event will occur, expressed by the ratio of the number of actual occurrences to the number of all possible outcomes.

After the discussion, express the definition of probability as an equation, and write it on the board:

Probability of event = P (event) = $\dfrac{\text{number of favorable outcomes}}{\text{number of possible outcomes}}$

Write another equation on the board:

P (tails) = $\dfrac{1 \text{ (number of favorable outcomes: tails)}}{2 \text{ (number of possible outcomes: heads or tails)}}$

Point out that the result of this equation can be expressed as a decimal (0.5) or a percent (50%). Discuss the meaning of other relevant terms such as "event," "experiment," and "outcome."

Small-group instruction (cooperative learning groups of 4–5 students): Ask students, "If you flip a coin 10 times, how many times would you predict that you would get tails?" (Answer: ½ of 10, or 5 times.)

Direct each group to flip a coin 10 times and record how many times tails comes up.

Ask students, "If you flip the coin 30 times, how many times will you get tails?" (Answer: ½ of 30, or 15 times.)

Direct each group to flip the coin 30 times and record the results.

Let students repeat the experiment, this time flipping 100 times.

REINFORCEMENT

Allow time for each group to share their results with the class. What trends do they notice in the results? (Answers will vary, but the general trend should be that the more times the coin is flipped, the closer the outcome gets to the prediction.)

To determine if students understand the ratio at work in probability, note whether or not they are able to convert the fractions from their experiments to the equivalent percents.

HOMEWORK

Instruct students to find two coins to use. They can be pennies, nickels, dimes, or quarters, but must be the same kind of coin. Instruct students to write down the following directions:

1. Flip each coin once. The possible outcomes for the two coins are heads/heads, heads/tails, tails/heads, tails/tails. What is the probability of both coins landing tails up?

2. Repeat the experiment, flipping both coins once. Does the opposite outcome—both coins landing heads up—occur ¼, or 25%, of the time?

Activity Sheet
Understanding Probability

1. Imagine that the following geometric figures are cut out and put in a bag. If you pull out a figure, what is the probability of selecting a square? _____

□ ○ □ ○ □ □

What is the probability of selecting a circle? _____

2. How many pairs of circles are there? _____

How many pairs of squares are there? _____

What is the total number of pairs? _____

If you randomly select a pair, what is the probability of selecting a pair of circles? _____

What is the probability of selecting a pair of squares? _____

How is the answer for problem 1 related to the answers for this problem?

_____

_____

3.   If you rearrange the letters in the word "MATH,"
     there are 24 possible outcomes (they won't be real
     words). List the 24 outcomes below. Don't forget to
     include "MATH" as your first outcome!

     _____

     _____

     _____

     _____

4.   If you rearrange the letters in the word "BOOK,"
     there are 10 outcomes (remember, they may not
     spell real words). List the 10 outcomes below,
     starting with "BOOK."

     _____

     _____

     _____

5.   There are four letters in the word "MATH" and four
     letters in the word "BOOK." Why is there a
     difference in the number of outcomes?

     _____

     _____

     _____

6. Sarah has three sweaters, one each in red, blue, and gray. She has five pairs of pants, one each in green, orange, black, blue, and pink. If she does not worry about matching colors, how many sweater-pants outfits can Sarah put together? _____

Does she have enough outfits for a 2-week vacation without wearing the same combination twice?
Yes / No (Circle one.)

Answers

1. Squares: $\frac{4}{6}$, $\frac{2}{3}$, .67, or 66%.
   Circles: $\frac{2}{6}$, $\frac{1}{3}$, .33, or 33%.

2. 1 pair of circles, 2 pairs of squares, 3 total pairs. Probability of selecting a pair of circles: $\frac{2}{6}$, $\frac{1}{3}$, .33, or 33%. Probability of selecting a pair of squares: $\frac{4}{6}$, $\frac{2}{3}$, .67, or 66%. The probability is the same.

3. MATH, MTHA, MTAH, MHTA, MHAT, MAHT
   AMTH, ATHM, AHTM, ATMH, AHMT, AMHT
   TMAH, TAMH, TMHA, TAHM, THAM, THMA
   HMAT, HAMT, HMTA, HATM, HTAM, HTMA

4. BOOK, BOKO, BKOO
   OBKO, OKBO, OOBK, OOKB
   KOOB, KOBO, KBOO

5. "BOOK" has fewer options because it only has three different letters.

6. She can make 15 different outfits, so yes, she has enough for 2 weeks.

Sample Science Lesson Plan, Grade 4

STATE STANDARD

Students will use scientific inquiry to pose questions, seek answers, and develop solutions.

AIM

To learn about the eating habits of barn owls and hawks.

SKILLS TAUGHT

Whole-language skills: Students will develop vocabulary ("predator," "prey," "dissection," "nocturnal," "birds of prey," "regurgitate," and "sterilize"), read aloud, and respond via complete sentence with answers to open-ended questions.

Critical thinking skills: Students will make comparative analysis.

Mathematical skills: Students will measure in centimeters and develop bar graphs.

Science skills: Students will dissect.

Technological skills: Students will practice keyboarding and using the Internet for research.

MOTIVATIONAL LEAD-IN

Display large colored posters of owls and hawks.

MATERIALS AND RESOURCES

Posters depicting owls and hawks, FOSS® Science Stories [Full Option Science System, published by Delta Education], computers, owl pellet study kits, magnifying glasses, toothpicks, unlined paper, rulers, and colored pens, pencils, or crayons

PROCEDURES

Whole-group instruction: Ask the students to read aloud excerpts from the FOSS Science Stories concerning the behaviors of owls and hawks. Students will then proceed to their computer stations to access more information about these birds via the Internet.

Pose open-ended questions to the students based on their findings. Direct students to respond in complete sentences.

Small-group instruction (4–5 students depending on class size): Give each group several sheets of unlined paper, toothpicks, a magnifying glass, and an owl pellet kit containing a study guide, regurgitated owl pellets, and instruments for dissection.

Direct students to dissect the pellets and measure, in centimeters, the contents of each pellet.

Help the groups make bar graphs of their individual pellet's contents. Owl pellets typically contain the skeletal remains of the small prey they eat since they are incapable of fully digesting the bones, teeth, claws, and feathers. Help students compare differences in their findings.

REINFORCEMENT

Ask a student from each group to report pellet contents and show bar-graph comparisons to the rest of the class.

HOMEWORK

Instruct students to use a computer or encyclopedia at home or at the library to research either owls or hawks to learn more. Ask them to write down facts and behaviors that weren't discussed in class.

Sample Integrated Mathematics and Science Lesson Plan, Grade 5

STATE STANDARD

Students will understand the relationships and common themes that connect mathematics, science, and technology, and apply the themes to these and other areas of learning.

AIM

To introduce key concepts of physics and enable students to understand how physics plays an important part in their daily lives.

SKILLS TAUGHT

Whole-language skills: Students will use the dictionary and develop vocabulary ("physics," "friction," "buoyancy," "adhesion," "cohesion," "lift," "energy," "matter," and "surface tension").

Critical thinking skills: Students will apply learned relationships between energy and matter to create practical projects in physics.

Mathematical skills: Students will measure, using metric and standard terms, and will create geometric shapes.

Science skills: Students will test and prove scientific concepts of energy and matter.

Technological skills: Students will practice keyboarding and using the Internet for research.

MOTIVATIONAL LEAD-IN

Ask for a volunteer to demonstrate a principle regarding buoyancy. A student will place a piece of wood and a large paper clip into a bowl of water. The piece of wood will float and the paper clip will sink, demonstrating that because wood contains air (which is lighter than water) and metal does not, the piece of wood is buoyant.

MATERIALS AND RESOURCES

Student dictionaries, computers, flat-bottomed metal pans, bowls, beakers of water, sheets of plastic, blow-dryers, ping-pong balls, small pieces of wood, and large paper clips

PROCEDURES

Whole-group instruction: Write the term "physics" on the board, and direct the students to look up its definition in their dictionaries. (Physics is the study of the relationship between energy and matter.) Then direct students to key in "physics" on their computers and find other information on the Internet. Discuss their Internet research and the dictionary definition.

Small-group instruction (cooperative learning groups, 4–5 students): Give each group separate projects that demonstrate the relationship between energy and matter. Facilitate each group's work.

Instruct one group to rub their palms briskly together until they experience heat as a result of *friction.*

Instruct another group to turn on blow-dryers at the cold setting, point them straight up, and hold a ping-pong ball in the airstream. As the balls hover in the air, the concept of *lift* will be demonstrated.

Instruct a third group to lay down a sheet of plastic, wet it, then place a flat-bottomed metal pan over the plastic. Students will demonstrate the concept of *adhesion* when they attempt to pull the pans straight up from the wet plastic: The plastic will stick to the pan.

REINFORCEMENT

Ask the students to discuss what they learned in this lesson. Present additional information to make sure that all of the key concepts and terms are included in the summary.

Discuss the definitions of "cohesion" and "surface tension" with students before assigning homework.

Cohesion: Intermolecular attraction between like molecules

Surface tension: The molecular force between particles within a body or substance that acts to unite them

Homework
Cohesion and Surface Tension

1. Fill a glass with water, then use your finger or a spoon to dribble a few separate drops of water on the outside of the glass. Watch the lines run together. Observe and write down your findings on *cohesion*.

    _____

    _____

    _____

    _____

    _____

    _____

    _____

2. Collect two paper clips and a bowl of water. Open one paper clip by unfolding the inner loop; it should look like an S. Place the other paper clip on the end of the S-clip, as if the S-clip were a spatula.

    Water and many other liquids behave as if they have a "skin" on the surface. It is this skin that supports the paper clip. The skin on liquids is caused by the inward pull on molecules at the surface, and this effect is called *surface tension*.

Slowly and gently, slide the paper clip from the S-clip to the bowl filled with water. Use care so that surface tension will hold the clip on top of the water. How do you know that the clip is not floating?

_____

_____

_____

_____

_____

_____

_____

3. Insert a second clip vertically in the water and let it go. Does it float?

This activity was adapted from McGrath, 1986, and Kerrod & Holgate, 2002.

Answers

1. Answers will vary.

2. If you press on the clip, it sinks. It doesn't have buoyancy. It won't float back up to the surface.

3. The second clip will not float if inserted vertically because it has been pushed past the surface of the water. There is no surface tension to hold it up.

Math and Science Lesson Plans That Work: Middle School

As some researchers have noted, "Given the emotional, physiological, and intellectual changes which children begin to experience as early as fifth grade, it is imperative to create some type of institution specially geared to meeting their individual needs" (Van Scotter, Kraft, & Hass, 1979, p. 267). This statement can serve as a rationale for developing a curriculum and teaching paradigm in math and science for middle-school children. Among other changes, during this stage children become more scientific in thinking: "As of eleven to twelve years, formal thinking becomes possible, i.e., the logical operations begin to be transported from the plane of concrete manipulation to the ideational plane, where they are expressed in some kind of language (words, mathematical symbols, etc.) without the support of perception, experience, or even faith" (Piaget, as quoted in Woolfolk, 2004, p. 32).

In other words, middle-school children have greater capacity to grasp the abstract. With respect to mathematics, children at this age are now ready to learn elementary algebra, introductory statistics, and the coordinate system. With respect to science, they can begin to grasp astronomy, electrical connections, and elementary chemistry. The following sample lessons explore these ideas.

Sample Mathematics Lesson Plan, Grade 6

STATE STANDARD

Students will understand mathematics and become mathematically confident by communicating and reasoning mathematically, by applying mathematics in real-world settings, and by solving problems through the integrated study of algebra.

AIM

To introduce the meaning of the term "equation" and demonstrate how to solve an equation using a form of math called "algebra."

SKILLS TAUGHT

Whole-language skills: Students will develop vocabulary ("algebra," "equation," "unknown," "product," and "quotient").

Critical thinking skills: Students will use a particular systematic process of solving an equation.

Mathematical skills: Students will add, subtract, multiply, and divide.

MOTIVATIONAL LEAD-IN

Draw the following diagram on the board:

Explain that on the left side of the diagram there are 4 visible coins and an unknown number of coins hidden behind the square.

Ask, "If the left side equals the right side, which has 7 visible coins, how many coins are hidden on the left side?"

MATERIALS

Paper, pencils, worksheets

PROCEDURES

Whole-group instruction: Explain that the coins hidden behind the square are called *unknowns* and state, "In algebra, the unknown is usually represented by the letter '*x*' or the letter '*y*.' We will use the letter '*n*.' Algebra is a branch of mathematics that uses letters and symbols in the place of unknown numbers."

Write the algebraic equation that represents the coin diagram on the board:

$$n + 4 = 7$$

Define the term "equation" as "a statement made up of numbers, letters, and symbols with left and right sides separated by an equal sign. One part of an algebraic equation has an unknown quantity, which we call *n*. In the equation, the equal sign (=) and the word 'is' mean the same thing. The equal sign shows that one side is the same as the other."

Then solve the equation. Following are some suggestions for explaining the solving process.

- "Solving an equation means finding out what *n* is. Sometimes this is called 'solving for *n*.' When we know what *n* is, we know what's called the *value* of *n*. The answer to a problem will always be *n* = a number."

- "Remember, an equation always has left and right sides separated by an equal sign. $n + 4 = 7$ is really another way of saying $7 = 7$. The goal of solving the equation is for the left side of the equation to have only *n*."

- "We are now ready for the second operation of the equation. We address the number '4' by subtracting it from both sides. Therefore, $n + 4 - 4 = 7 - 4$."

- "Plus 4 and minus 4 equal 0."

- "We are now ready to solve the equation and find the value of n." Write on the board:

$$n + 4 \ = \ 7$$
$$-4 \ = \ -4$$
$$\overline{}$$
$$n + 0 \ = \ 3$$
$$\text{Answer: } n \ = \ 3$$

- "To solve for n, we always reverse the operation in the equation. If the equation were $n - 4 = 7$, what should we do? We would add 4 to both sides."

Proceed to a second example showing the algebraic notation for multiplication. Write on the board:

$$5n = 20$$

Explain to the class, "This equation states that 5 multiplied by n or 5 times n is 20. To solve, we reverse the operation from multiplication to division." Note that the multiplication sign of "x" is not used in algebra, since letters are used to represent the unknown. Review the various ways that multiplication is represented in algebra.

Then return to the equation at hand. Write on the board:

$$5n \div 5 \ = \ 20 \div 5$$
$$\text{or}$$
$$5n \,/\, 5 \ = \ 20 \,/\, 5$$
$$\text{or}$$
$$\frac{5n}{5} \ = \ \frac{20}{5}$$

$$\text{Answer: } n \ = \ 4$$

Note that, "Beyond knowing that $n = 4$, we also know that 5 x 4 = 20."

Small-group instruction (3 or 4 students per group): Instruct each group to find the value of n in the following equations:

$$n + 3 \; = \; 7$$

$$n + 5 \; = \; 9$$

$$n + 1 \; = \; 10$$

Whole-group instruction: After small groups have solved the above equations, return to whole-group instruction. Write on the board a more complex equation that involves two different kinds of operations:

$$3n + 4 \; = \; 19$$

Then solve the equation. Following are some suggestions for explaining the solving process.

- "Solving an equation that involves two kinds of mathematical processes, like adding *and* multiplying, is like unwrapping a package. When you are unwrapping a package, you take off the outer layers of paper first. When you are solving a complex equation, you do the same thing: You reverse the order of all operations or steps, starting with addition and subtraction."

- "$3n + 4 = 19$ means that 3 multiplied by n plus 4 is 19. Remember, in an algebraic equation, 3 multiplied by n can be expressed in three ways." Write on the board:

$$3 \cdot n$$

$$3(n)$$

$$3n$$

- "The first thing we do is reverse the order of operations." Write on the board:

$$3n + 4 = 19$$
$$-4 = -4$$
$$\overline{}$$
$$3n = 15$$

- "Let's unwrap this package. The last step of our equation was '+ 4.' We must remove it to find the value of $3n$ before 4 was added. If we subtract 4 from both sides of the equation, we will be left with $3n$ on the left and 15 on the right."

- "Although we have started to unwrap the package, the process is not complete. We must now reverse the operation of multiplication by using the operation of division." Write on the board:

$$3n \div 3 = 15 \div 3$$
$$\text{or}$$
$$3n / 3 = 15 / 3$$
$$\text{or}$$
$$\frac{3n}{3} = \frac{15}{3}$$

Answer: $n = 5$

- "The package is completely unwrapped!"

REINFORCEMENT

Ask the students to review the definitions of the terms "algebra," "equation," and "unknown." Ask them to explain the process of solving the equations discussed in the day's lesson.

HOMEWORK

Distribute the handouts "Algebraic Equations" (page 141) and "Building an Algebraic Vocabulary" (page 143).

Algebraic Equations

Solve these six equations. Not all answers will be whole numbers. Remember to show your work!

1. $n + 3 = 20$

    _____

    _____

2. $n + 11 = 55$

    _____

    _____

3. $n + 4 = 10$

    _____

    _____

4. $4n + 1 = 39$

    _____

    _____

5. $3n + 6 = 21$

    _____

    _____

6. $6n + 0 = 45$

    _____

    _____

Answers

1. 17

2. 44

3. 6

4. 9.5

5. 5

6. 7.5

Building an Algebraic Vocabulary

Some of the operations used in arithmetic are written differently when we start to write algebra. For instance, 5•*n*, 5*n*, and 5(*n*) all mean "5 times the value of n."

The formula **5 + *n*** can also be written ***n* + 5** and means "5 increased by *n*" or "5 more than *n*." Similarly, "6 less than *n*" or "*n* decreased by 6" is written *n* – 6 and "*n* divided by 4" is written ***n*/4.**

Directions: Connect each of the following statements to the algebraic equation that expresses the same mathematical question. Write in the letter of the matching equation.

___ 1. nine increased by a number   a. 5 + *n*

___ 2. five more than a number   b. 2*n*

___ 3. seven less than a number   c. *n* + 3

___ 4. twice a number   d. *n* + 9

___ 5. five times a number   e. 3*n*

___ 6. the result when nine is   f. *n* – 2
    multiplied by a number

___ 7. the product of three and   g. 6/*n*
    a number

___ 8. the number less two   h. *n* + 6 = 8

___ 9. the sum of the number and three   i. *n* – 7

___ 10. six divided by the number   j. 9*n*

___ 11. the sum of a number and six
    is eight

k. $5n$

___ 12. eight less than the number
    is twelve

l. $5n + 4 = 24$

___ 13. eight times the number
    is twenty-four

m. $8n = 24$

___ 14. the product of eight and
    the number is seventy-two

n. $n - 8 = 12$

___ 15. five times a number increased
    by four is twenty-four

o. $8n = 72$

Answers

1. d

2. a

3. i

4. b

5. k

6. j

7. e

8. f

9. c

10. g

11. h

12. n

13. m

14. o

15. l

Sample Science Lesson Plan, Grade 6

STATE STANDARD

Students will use scientific inquiry to pose questions, seek answers, and develop solutions.

AIM

To understand what happens during a solar eclipse and a lunar eclipse.

SKILLS TAUGHT

Whole-language skills: Students will develop vocabulary ("eclipse," "lunar," "lunar eclipse," "orbit," "penumbra," "solar," "solar eclipse," and "umbra").

Science skills: Students will learn about the locations of the sun, moon, and Earth during solar and lunar eclipses. Students will interpret data about solar and lunar eclipses by using models.

MOTIVATIONAL LEAD-IN

Turn on the projector, and turn off the lights. Put your hand in front of the projector's light to create a shadow on the screen. Ask how a shadow is created.

MATERIALS AND RESOURCES

Projector, dowel rods, small and large foam balls, four lamps with 100-watt bulbs

PROCEDURES

Whole-group instruction: Turn the lights back on. Write "eclipse" on the board, and define it as "the darkness resulting from blocking a beam of light with an object, thus creating a shadow." Then explain that when the moon blocks the sun's light and casts its shadow on Earth, that is a *solar* eclipse. During a solar eclipse, the moon does not completely cover the sun, and a blurred shadow is produced. The dark middle of the shadow is the umbra, and the light ring around the edge is the penumbra (Kerrod & Holgate, 2002).

Then explain that a lunar eclipse happens "when the moon moves through the Earth's shadow. During this event the moon becomes red rather than completely dark," due to the angled sunlight (Kerrod & Holgate, 2002, p. 104). Draw the following diagrams on the board.

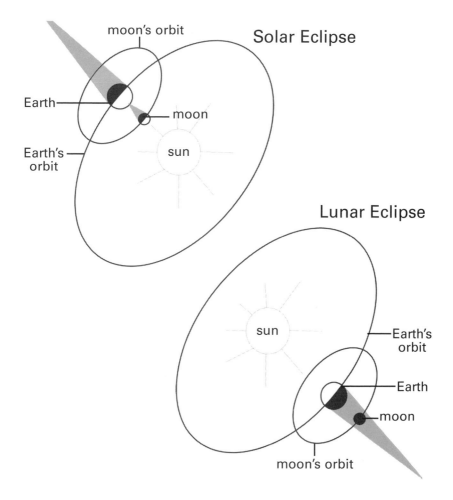

Small-group instruction (3–4 students): Cluster groups around the lamps. Give each group two dowel rods and two foam balls (one small, one large), and ask them to push a dowel into each ball. Explain that the large ball will represent the Earth, the small ball will represent the moon, and the lamp will represent the sun. Turn on the lamps, and turn out the overhead lights.

Direct each group to use one model to cast a shadow on the other model. Explain that when these shadows fall, an eclipse occurs. Ask students to show the moon's shadow falling on Earth. Ask, "Why do you think this is called a *solar* eclipse?"

Then ask students to arrange their models so that Earth's shadow falls on the moon, and point out that this is the model of a lunar eclipse. Ask, "Where were the sun, Earth, and the moon located during our two experiments?"

REINFORCEMENT

Ask students from each group to explain what happens during a lunar eclipse and a solar eclipse. Ask other students to define "penumbra," "umbra," and "orbit."

HOMEWORK

Ask students to copy down the diagrams of eclipses from the board, and to explain them in writing, based on what they learned during the day's lesson.

This lesson was adapted from Community School District 17, 1995.

Sample Mathematics Lesson Plan, Grade 7

STATE STANDARD

Students will use mathematical analysis as appropriate to pose questions, test assumptions, seek answers, and develop solutions.

AIM

To introduce the meaning of the term "statistics" and show students how statistics play an important part in our daily lives.

SKILLS TAUGHT

Whole-language skills: Students will develop vocabulary ("statistics," "data," "interval," "mean," "median," "mode," and "range").

Critical thinking skills: Students will analyze data.

Mathematical skills: Students will calculate measures of central tendency (mean, median, and mode) and find the range of a set of numbers. They will practice adding, dividing, and rounding off numbers.

MOTIVATIONAL LEAD-IN

Ask students to name a star basketball player, and ask if anyone knows how many points he or she averages in a season. Then ask the students to choose a favorite song, and ask how many times, on average, this song plays on the radio during a week. Explain that there is a form of mathematics called *statistics*, and the term "average" is called the "mean" in statistics.

MATERIALS AND RESOURCES

Overhead projector, transparencies, handouts, calculators

PROCEDURES

Whole-group instruction: Distribute the handout "Statistical Terms" (page 151), and discuss each term with the class.

Instruct the students how to calculate the mean for the scores made by the basketball player and the mean for a favorite song played on the radio during the week.

Small-group instruction (cooperative learning groups of 4–5 students): Distribute the handout "Calculating Averages" (page 152). Instruct students to find the following information: data, median, mode, and range.

REINFORCEMENT

Ask students from each group to explain the meaning of "statistics," "data," "mean," "median," "mode," and "range."

Statistical Terms

Statistics: A form of mathematics that deals with the collection, analysis, and interpretation of numerical data.

Addend: A number to be added to another.

Data: Recorded information gathered by observation, questioning, or measurement.

Frequency: How often something occurs.

Interval: A set of numbers that ranges between two numbers (a and b), possibly including a or b.

Mean: A number found by dividing the sum of two or more numbers by the number of addends (also called the average).

Median: The number in the middle when you list the numbers of a data set in numerical order (least to greatest or greatest to least). If you have an even amount of numbers, then it is an average of the two middle numbers.

Mode: The number that appears most often in a data set. Sometimes there is no mode, and sometimes there is more than one.

Range: The difference between the smallest and largest number in the data set.

Calculating Averages

Calculating a Basketball Player's Average

A basketball player's average indicates the average points per game that he or she earns. You can find the player's average by dividing the total number of points he or she earned in a season by the number of games in the season.

Number of Points Player Earns per Game

Game 1:   15

Game 2:   25

Game 3:   30

Game 4:   20

Game 5:   19

Game 6:   33

Game 7:   12

Game 8:   17

Game 9:   23

Game 10: 27

If we add up all the points (the **addends**), the total is 221.

If we divide 221 by the number of games (10), the result represents the player's average or **mean** points per game: 22.1, or 22 if we round to the nearest whole number.

This equation is represented mathematically as:

Sum of Addends / Number of Addends = Mean

221/10 =22.1

Calculating Daily Play Rates

We can use the same process to determine the average number of times in a day that a radio station plays a certain song.

Number of Times Station Plays Song per Day

Day 1:	4
Day 2:	3
Day 3:	3
Day 4:	5
Day 5:	3
Day 6:	4
Day 7:	4

The equation for determining the average or **mean** number of times the song is played is:

$$26/7 = n$$

Thus, during a week, the favorite song is played a mean of 3.5 times a day, or 4, when rounded to the nearest ones.

Understanding Statistics

After many years of buying her ugly outfits that she hated, Meredith's parents finally decided to allow her to pick out her own skating outfit. They asked her to research prices on various possibilities and summarize her findings. Then the family could decide together what to purchase.

Meredith found eight outfits that she really liked. The prices of the outfits, from the first store to the last store, were $32, $11, $8, $66, $52, $68, $32, and $19. Please help Meredith summarize her findings!

1. The range in prices is $_____.

2. The mean price is $_____.

3. _____% of the prices were more than $52.

4. The median price is $_____.

5. The modal price is $_____.

6. Twenty-five percent of the prices were less than $_____.

7. If Meredith's parents decided to give her the mean amount to make her purchase, how much more money would she need to buy the most expensive outfit? _____

8. Meredith could purchase at least _____ of her outfits with the mean price. In other words, what is the number of outfits priced less than or equal to the mean price?

Meredith's father is offering her the mean, plus an additional 1/3 of the mean, if she cleans the barbeque grill. Meredith's mother offered her an additional 2/5 of the mean if she cleans her George Foreman® grill.

9. She would get a total of $_____ from her mother, or a total of $_____ from her father.

10. Meredith should take both jobs, because this would increase her mean amount by _____%. With this increase, will Meredith be able to buy the most expensive outfit? Yes / No (Circle one.)

11. If not, the most expensive outfit that she could buy would be $_____. After buying that outfit, how many additional outfits will she be able to buy with the remaining money? (Circle one):

    0   1   2   3   4   5

12. Sheila, Meredith's best friend, found out that each of Meredith's outfits has been increased by $4. The prices are now $36, $15, $12, $70, $56, $72, $36, and $23. The mean price is $_____ now. It has increased / decreased (circle one) by $_____.

13. The range of the new prices is _____.
    Compared to the old range, the new range shows:
    an increase / a decrease / no change (circle one).

14. If each original price, on the other hand, were
    decreased by $5, the mean should be decreased /
    increased (circle one) by $_____. The new
    mean would be $_____.

Answers

1. 60

2. 36

3. 25%

4. 32

5. 32

6. 19

7. $32.00

8. 5

9. $50.40, $48

10. 73.33%; no.

11. $52; 1 outfit.

12. $40; it has increased by $4.

13. $60; no change.

14. The mean should be decreased by $5, to $31.

Sample Mathematics Lesson Plan, Grade 8

STATE STANDARD

Students will understand mathematics and become mathematically confident by communicating and reasoning mathematically, by applying mathematics in real-world settings, and by solving problems through the integrated study of number systems and algebra.

AIM

To teach students how to determine the value of two unknowns by graphing an equation.

SKILLS TAUGHT

Whole-language skills: Students will develop vocabulary ("graph," "axis," "coordinates," "plotting," and "origin").

Critical thinking skills: Students will use the relationship of two variables to measure their respective value.

Math skills: Students will plot coordinates and develop equations.

Technological skills: Students will visit Internet websites to increase their graphing skills.

MOTIVATIONAL LEAD-IN

Kevin and Tom are best friends. They decide to go to the movies on Saturday. Their tickets will cost a total of $20. Between them, the boys have $20 for the tickets, but what amount does each boy have?

MATERIALS

Paper, pencils, graph paper, rulers, computers

PROCEDURES

Whole-group instruction: Distribute graphing paper and the handout on graphing vocabulary (see page 163). Explain and discuss the eight terms on the handout.

Open the discussion by asking students how they might form an equation that expresses the problem:

- "If we don't know what either Kevin or Tom has, but we know they have $20 together, how could we express that as an equation?"

Ask students to give you six possible combinations that add up to $20. Write these on the board, along with the equation $x + y = 20$. These might include $4 + 16 = 20$, $10 + 10 = 20$, $5 + 15 = 20$, $1 + 19 = 20$, $2 + 18 = 20$, and $13 + 7 = 20$.

Explain that a graph can show all possible solutions to the equation $x + y = 20$. Describe how x and y are referred to as "coordinates" in graphing and are written as (x, y). Write on the board:

$$(x, y)$$

or

(amount Kevin has, amount Tom has)

Take the students' suggested values for x and y, and write them in coordinate form, such as:

Kevin has $4, Tom has $16

is the same as

$$(4, 16)$$

Review the importance of maintaining a consistent order. Explain that although the values of x and y are variable, the letters must always stand for the same boy, and their placement in the equation should remain constant:

- "In an algebraic equation, x comes before y, just as it does in the alphabet. When we use the coordinate system, (x, y) must always mean (Kevin, Tom), not (Tom, Kevin).The example of (4, 16) means that Kevin has $4 and Tom has $16. If we change the coordinates to (16, 4), Kevin has $16 and Tom has $4."

Discuss the relationship between what algebra calls an unknown, and what the coordinate system calls a variable. Review the definitions of both, and write them on the board.

Once students have grasped these concepts, turn to graphing.

- "There are so many solutions to this problem that we would not be able to list all of them. We can graph our coordinates to create a kind of picture that shows all possible solutions."

Pass out a handout or use an overhead projector to show students what a graph looks like.

Explain:

- "A coordinate system uses two lines that form a 90-degree angle. The point at which they meet is called the *origin*. The line going from left to right is always called the *x*-axis. The line going up and down is always called the *y*-axis."

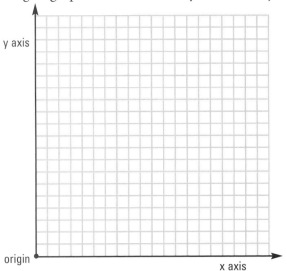

Then describe how coordinates like (*x*, *y*) describe points along the *x*-axis and *y*-axis. Mark and number regular intervals along the axes. Note that the coordinates of the origin are (0,0).

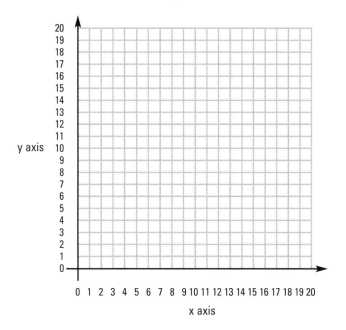

- "The locations of *x* and *y* are based on directions given within the parenthesis of (*x*, *y*). The *x* tells you to go left or right of the origin, and *y* tells you to go up or down from the origin."

Show students how certain coordinates would be plotted.

- "Let's go back to our six possible numerical combinations that show how Kevin's amount (*x*) and Tom's amount (*y*) could add up to $20. We will graph or *plot* these solutions by connecting the points with a ruler."

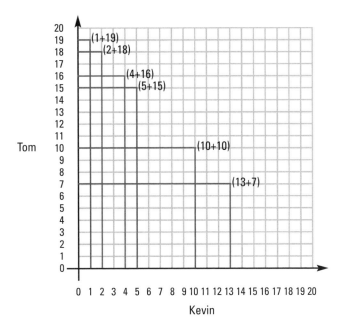

Small-group instruction (cooperative learning groups of 4–5 students): Pass out graph paper, and guide students through the process of drawing the *x*-axis and *y*-axis and marking regular intervals from 1 to 20. Then instruct them to plot other solutions for Kevin and Tom. Write on the board:

(12, 8)   (0, 20)   (20, 0)   (6, 14)   (11, 9)

REINFORCEMENT

Ask the students to explain "variables," "graphing function," "axis," "coordinates," "plotting," and "origin."

HOMEWORK

Ask students to use the process they learned in class to find and plot five possible solutions for the equation x + y = 10.

Graphing Vocabulary

Graph: A diagram that shows the relationship between two sets of numbers.

Axis: On a graph, there is an x axis (the horizontal line) and a y axis (the vertical line). The plural of "axis" is "axes."

Coordinates: Two numbers that determine an exact position of a point. The first number represents the location along the x axis, and the second number represents the location along the y axis. When we draw lines from those numbers, the lines intersect at the point corresponding to the coordinates.

Unknown: A quantity represented in an equation by a letter (such as x, y, or n). The value of that letter is not revealed until the equation is solved, so it is called an unknown.

Variable: Another term for "unknown."

Plotting: Determining and marking points on graph paper using coordinates.

Origin: The starting point at which the x and y axes meet or intersect. Its coordinates are (0,0).

Equation: A statement made up of numbers, letters, and symbols with left and right sides separated by an equal sign. One part of an algebraic equation has an unknown quantity, which we call x. In the equation, the equal symbol (=) and the word "is" mean the same thing. The equal sign shows that one side is the same as the other.

Understanding the Coordinate System

1. Tonya (*x*) and Shanai (*y*) are best friends. They decide to go to the circus on Saturday. The tickets for both girls will cost $30. Between them, they have $30 for the tickets, but what amount does each girl have? Write the equation that expresses this problem.

   _____

   _____

2. List ten possible answers for the above question.

   _____

   _____

   _____

   _____

   _____

   _____

3. Use your graph paper and the coordinate system to plot your answers. Then use the graph to show all possible solutions.

4. With respect to Tonya and Shanai, what do the expressions below mean?

   (17, 13)

   (14, 16)

   (15, 15)

   (12, 18)

The Role of Families and Care Providers

Families and care providers are integral parts of a child's math and science learning process. Since the mid-20th century, significant research, publications, and government intervention have supported family involvement in schools. After the passage of the Federal Elementary and Secondary Education Act of 1965 (which created compensatory programs for disadvantaged children), the New York City Board of Education created Title I parent advisory councils. Under the No Child Left Behind Act of 2001, Title I was amended to extend provisions for comprehensive parent involvement throughout the entire country (U.S. Department of Education, 2002).

In *Worlds Apart: Relationships Between Families and Schools,* Harvard sociologist Sara Lawrence-Lightfoot proposed the following considerations for building positive alliances between families and schools (Lawrence-Lightfoot, 1978):

- Families teach children certain skills at home that have transferability into school, such as organization, independence, and assertiveness.

- To provide a productive and comfortable environment for students, schools must meaningfully incorporate the familial and cultural skills and values that children have already learned in their homes and communities.

- Children learn and grow in schools where parents and teachers share a similar vision and collaborate in guiding students forward.

- A working collaboration of parents and teachers not only transforms the educational environment and cultural medium of the school, but also changes parents' and teachers' perceptions of their roles and relationships.

James Comer (1988), the creator of a successful intervention project at Yale University's Child Study Center, pointed out that schools must win the support of parents and learn to respond to the needs of students in creative ways. A significant portion of his intervention project was devoted to building supportive bonds that draw together children, parents, and schools.

Comer's program produced significant results. Fourth graders from two schools in New Haven, Connecticut made steady gains in mathematics from 1964 to 1984. In Prince George County, Maryland, 10 schools with primarily African-American student populations used the Comer program and made larger average percentile gains from 1958 to 1987 on California Achievement Test scores (particularly in mathematics) than the school district as a whole (Comer, 1988). This success has been duplicated at more than 50 schools around the country.

Using Math and Science at Home

Teachers can start to involve families in their children's math and science education by showing them how to create simple tasks or use ordinary household activities to teach concepts in math and science. At each grade level, as teachers add more homework tasks, they can also increase the number of assisted family tasks.

Educators should recognize families and their children when they reinforce learning at home. Recognition can be as simple as presenting certificates on a monthly or bimonthly basis, depending on class size. These certificates should include the names of the child and the participating family member or care provider.

Math Tasks

Teachers can alert families to math tasks they can perform with their children, many of which are simple and fun variations on things they already do together. For example, young children often learn how to count to 10 during the year before kindergarten. Families can be instrumental in helping them relate numbers to objects, an important early learning experience, by asking them to count particular objects: one crayon, two crayons, three crayons, and so on. Simultaneously, the symbols for the cardinal numbers 1 through 10 can be illustrated. Care providers can teach the concept of ordinal numbers by simply lining family members up and expressing who is first, second, third, and so forth. In these ways and more, families can be shown how to teach children not just a string of numbers, but also the *significance* of each number.

Parents generally ask their children to assist them in selected household tasks. Why not make those tasks mathematical experiences? Younger children, for example, can be instructed to make sure that there are a total of four plates on the table, or asked to sort items into groups so that each family member has one plate, one napkin, two forks, one spoon, one glass, and so forth. Games can also be turned into subtle mathematical experiences: In hide-and-seek, children can count by fives or tens instead of ones; musical chairs can make subtraction easy to see and understand.

Older children can be given more complex mathematical tasks as part of everyday family life. Consider the following possibilities:

- Give children a fixed budget for school clothes, and ask them to comparison shop to learn how much they can buy if they buy designer clothes, ordinary clothes, or thrift-store clothes.

- Have children help rearrange furniture by first creating to-scale drawings on graph paper of the room and each object in it.

- Use the stock-market page of the newspaper to practice adding and subtracting fractions, as when a stock moves from 57¾ to 57⅞, for example.

- Use wrenches to teach the relative size of fractions: If the ⁵⁄₁₆" wrench is too small and the ½" wrench is too big, which wrench should be tried next?

Science Tasks

The kitchen is an ideal arena for many science activities. Even young children can assist with simple tasks like measuring ingredients for recipes; this introduces counting as well as the concept of measurement and its different forms: weight versus volume, dry volume versus wet volume, metric versus U.S. system. Parents can talk about the sources of ingredients (eggs come from chickens, flour from comes from a plant called wheat, different cooking oils come from corn, olives, sunflower seeds, and so on). Parents can use a whole-language approach to describe the texture of various ingredients and introduce vocabulary like "liquid," "solid," "powdery," "oily," and so on.

Baking, frying, and broiling can provide many examples of the science of biochemistry. Applying heat to a mixture of raw food elements results in a chemical change; consuming and digesting food also creates chemical changes. Bread and cakes become light and fluffy due to the presence of yeast, baking powder, or egg whites. Fermentation and aging produce wine, cheese, and mold—the source of penicillin.

Good health is a requisite to educational success; therefore, excellent lessons on biology and good nutrition can take place in the kitchen. Families can:

- Discuss the variety of sources from which proteins, vitamins, and minerals can be obtained, beyond red meats, pork, and starches.

- Discuss the role of too much sugar, salt, and fat in the increase of health problems like type-2 diabetes and obesity, and identify nourishing foods and healthy choices.

- Enlist children in comparative shopping for groceries (particularly in inner-city areas, where food can be expensive) and in preparing food by a variety of methods.

Parents can also make connections between school and their children's hobbies. If students are learning about the three different types of rocks in school—sedimentary, igneous, and metamorphic— parents can encourage children to collect rocks in and around their community and label them in one of the three categories.

Reinforcing School Lessons

Families are best able to reinforce the actual content of school lessons when they can help children with homework. To that end, teachers should give children a math and science homework schedule each Friday for the following week and instruct them to share this schedule with their parents. This strategy will give families an opportunity to schedule time to assist their children with homework.

Sometimes homework is ignored at home because parents are not sure of the homework's objectives or do not understand the homework's questions. Homework schedules and school orientations will help alleviate family insecurities. Parents talented in math and science can be trained to teach other parents how to help their children with homework assignments. Parents weaker in these subjects may be able to receive tutoring assistance. Some schools provide parent education for assisting children with homework.

Repetition as a reinforcement activity plays a significant part of the learning process, particularly among at-risk learners, and therefore should be employed at home. Schools should assist in preparing families to render efficient home reinforcement. Family workshops conducted by the school or district can provide specific reinforcement tasks and activities.

Building Good Study Habits

Following are some basic ways that families and care providers can help children build the study habits necessary for success in math and science. These habits become very important as the difficulty of the subject matter increases at each grade level. Teachers should work with families to prepare them to:

- Encourage children to review the day's lessons every evening for at least 15 to 20 minutes. Families should set aside a specific time for review, even if there is no assigned homework for the night.

- Show children how to read a textbook effectively by explaining how to identify the main idea of a paragraph, what the relationship is between topics and subtopics, and why chapter summaries provided in the textbook are important.

- Discuss with children the seriousness of homework: that homework is a vital part of the studying and learning process, and should be completed with great care to ensure more performance accuracy on tests.

Reducing Test Anxiety

Teachers can also work with families to reduce students' test anxiety by encouraging them to:

- Guide children through regular review sessions. As part of the studying process, review builds self-confidence and reduces test anxiety.

- Go over actual test items from old tests so that children can practice and become used to the standardized form of testing (including filling in circles with a No. 2 pencil), the variety of questions (essay, multiple choice, fill in the blank, and so on), and the need to balance speed with accuracy.

- Help children to relax the evening before a test, go to bed early, and eat a light breakfast in the morning.

Challenges for Families of At-Risk Students

Today, there are many young parents who have not completed their high school education. Schools, therefore, must not only educate at-risk children more effectively in the classroom, but also find a way to make their parents proficient enough to assist in the education of their children. If this process occurs, the family-school partnership can become a reality.

Family workshops geared toward helping at-risk children can be supported by Title I funds that enable low-socioeconomic-status parents in urban and suburban areas to become more involved in the school and their children's educational development, through school workshops, the development of parent resources, and other parental development programs. Many after-school, community resource, and homework helper programs are sponsored by teacher unions, parent-teacher associations, and local religious institutions.

When families believe that they play an important part in the education of their children, their motivation is reinforced when children begin to make progress. There is nothing as rewarding for families as letting friends know that their children are doing well in school—and that they played a key role in their children's success.

Sample Science Unit, Adaptable for Grades 4–6

The following sample science unit illustrates how long-range thematic planning can encompass many tasks that help upper-elementary and middle-school children develop their critical thinking skills. The goals described within this lesson can be incorporated into daily lesson plans, allowing flexibility in the timeframe.

Theme: We Need One Another— The Wonderful Partnership of Plants, Aminals, and Humans (3- to 6-week unit)

STATE STANDARD

Students will apply technological knowledge and skills to design, construct, use, and evaluate products and systems to satisfy human and environmental needs.

MATERIALS AND RESOURCES

Outdoor trees and indoor potted plants; fertilizer, potting soil, soil, wood planks, rope; computers and software about animals, insects, and plant life; encyclopedias and relevant reference books; magazines, posters, and charts about animals, insects, and plant life; local colleges, departments of biology and/or ecology; local museums

Goal 1: Students will understand the origin of plant life.

Objective A: *Students will be able to identify common indoor and outdoor plants and trees.*

ACTIVITIES

- Students will conduct identification research of five common indoor plants using the Internet, video software, and encyclopedias and other reference books.

- Students will conduct identification research on five outdoor plants and/or trees using the Internet, video software, and encyclopedias and other reference books.

- Students will develop a journal to identify indoor and outdoor plants using common name, phylum, class, order, family, genus, species, and subspecies.

FORMATIVE EVALUATIONS

- Whole-class oral reviews that reinforce the main ideas of class lessons

- Weekly self-graded quizzes

- Analysis of the quality of each identification journal with timely feedback

Objective B*: Students will understand the importance of further research on indoor and outdoor plant life.*

ACTIVITIES

- Students will make field-trip observations at a plant nursery, a botanical garden, and a state park.

- Class discussions will be conducted on the results of field-trip observations.

- A local college professor of ecology will be invited to talk to students about the importance of specific plants to the general environment.

FORMATIVE EVALUATIONS

- Analysis of the quality of students' completed homework assignments

- Student self-evaluation via rubrics

- Whole-class oral reviews that reinforce the objectives of the lesson

Goal 2: Students will research and plan an actual garden.

Objective A: *Students will be able to understand the construction and designs of completed gardens.*

ACTIVITIES

- Students will make scientific inquiries into various types of gardens.

- Students will observe the initial growth of garden plants (potted indoors) with respect to amounts of sunlight, water, and other nutrients.

- Applying geometric mathematical principles, students will draw various garden designs.

- Applying geometric mathematical principles, students will construct a to-scale model garden.

FORMATIVE EVALUATION

- Peer evaluation via cooperative learning groups

Objective B: *Students will be able to make decisions on the actual spatial layout of a proposed garden.*

ACTIVITIES

- Students will make a field trip within the immediate community to find an area suitable for a garden location.

- Students will clean and prepare the site for planting.

FORMATIVE EVALUATIONS

- Quiz on life cycles of specific plants

- Peer evaluation via cooperative learning groups on fertilizing, watering, and sunlight

- Student self-evaluation via rubrics

Goal 3: Students will create a garden.

Objective A: *Students will acquire materials and resources necessary for the design and layout of a garden.*

ACTIVITIES

- Students will make field trips to plant nurseries and home improvement stores for donations of soil, planks, rope, and other necessary materials.

- Using the scale-model garden as a point of reference, students will apply arithmetic and geometric principles to measure and cordon off plots.

FORMATIVE EVALUATIONS

- Assessment of the quantity and quality of materials received as a result of student solicitations

- Assessment of the mathematical precision of the garden layout and design

Objective B: *Students will understand the importance of sunlight, water, and other nutrients in the development of healthy plants.*

ACTIVITIES

- Students will spread soil and add measured amounts of fertilizer and water in preparation for planting.

- Students will plant seeds, bulbs, tubers, and potted plants into designated plots.

- Students will access further information concerning the growth and care of these plants from the Internet.

SUMMATIVE EVALUATION

The extent to which Goals 1, 2, and 3 have been met can be measured through a final examination or a culminating activity (such as the development of the garden itself). The process of meeting the challenges of the culminating activities serves to reinforce the learning of all goals and objectives created by this 3- to 6-week experience.

Notes on the Unit Plan

A completed unit could have embraced a fourth goal as well: "Students will understand and appreciate the importance of plant life to humans and to the ecosystem." Incorporated within this goal would have been:

- An understanding of the importance of the process of photosynthesis

- An understanding of the relationships among plants, humans, animals, and insects

- Learning about the contributions that specific plants—such as aloe, grass, and oak and maple trees—make toward humans and other animals

Though the unit theme is about science, mathematics is integrated throughout various segments of the unit. Students can be taught, for example, how to apply arithmetic and geometrical principles by drawing various garden designs and constructing a to-scale garden plan using the geometric principles. This could be a summative-culminating activity.

This unit is designed for middle-school children, but it is adaptable to elementary grades. Drawing a garden design, for example, would be interesting and challenging to a fourth-grade class, since 8-, 9-, and 10-year-old children would be able to understand geometric shapes, angles, and symmetry. They are also able to draw simple maps and understand the use of parallel and perpendicular lines (coordinates) to plot locations. Fifth and sixth graders, with the assistance of sound teaching, would be able to create a to-scale garden plan by applying principles of measurement and using lines, angles, and circles.

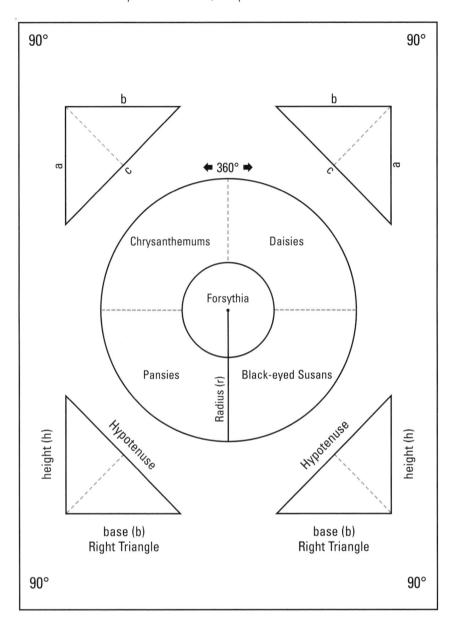

90°   90°

b   b

a   c   ← 360° →   c   a

Chrysanthemums   Daisies

Forsythia

Pansies   Black-eyed Susans

Radius (r)

height (h)   Hypotenuse   Hypotenuse   height (h)

base (b)   base (b)
Right Triangle   Right Triangle

90°   90°

Geometric Principles

- $a^2 + b^2 = c^2$ (Pythagorean Theorem)
- $A = \pi r^2$ (area of a circle)
- $A = \frac{1}{2} bh$ (area of a triangle)

Websites for Math and Science Reinforcement

■ ■

Math

A+ Math: www.aplusmath.com (grades 6–8)
Offers interactive math activities to help students improve their math skills and includes printable worksheets, the Homework Helper, and Flashcard Creator.

About.com: math.about.com (parents and educators, grades 6–8)
Provides guidance for parents who want to help their children with math.

Algebra.help: www.algebrahelp.com (grades 6–8)
Explains basics of algebra. Frequented by students and adults wanting to brush up.

Fun Mathematics Lessons: math.rice.edu/~lanius/Lessons (grades K–8)
Provides fun math activities for teachers to use in their lesson plans and interactive online math activities for students.

Interactive Mathematics Miscellany and Puzzles: www.cut-the-knot.org/algebra.shtml (grades 7–8)
Offers engaging mathematics for teachers, parents, and students.

The Math Arcade:
www.funbrain.com/brain/MathBrain/MathBrain.html
(grades 6–8)
Includes 25 math-based interactive games for students to play.

The Math Forum: mathforum.org (grades 5–8)
Offers question-and-answer email service for students, resources
for parents, and links to other math sites.

The Math League: mathleague.com/help/help.htm (grades 4–8)
Offers help on math topics such as fractions, whole numbers, basic
algebra, geometry and more.

Maths Net: Interctive Algebra: www.mathsnet.net/algebra
(grades 6–8)
Helps the student develop a better understanding of algebraic
equations through a variety of interactive algebra lessons using
"drag and drop" applets that allow the user to see the effect these
changes have.

Mr. Veasey's Interactive Algebra:
www.veazeys.com/math/lessons.htm (grades 6–8)
Provides randomly generated algebra problems and shows how to
reach the answers.

Mrs. Glosser's Math Goodies™: www.mathgoodies.com
(grades K–8)
Provides lessons, puzzles, and worksheets for students, educators,
and parents.

Plane Math: www.planemath.com/planemathmain.html (grades 6–8)
Connects math to airplanes; a cooperative project with NASA. Includes activities for students and information for parents and teachers.

Science

ActionBioscience.org: www.actionbioscience.org/lessondirectory.html (educators, grades K–12)
Offers a variety of scientific articles and lessons. Topics include bacteria (friend or foe?), biodiversity, real-life aliens (introduced species), ecosystems, global warming, biotechnology, genetically modified foods, and more.

The Miami Museum of Science: The Atoms Family: www.miamisci.org/af/sln/index.html (grades K–12)
Offers an online library that allows students to learn science and try out physics experiments with famous tour guides from old movies, including Dracula, Frankenstein, and the Wolf Man.

Penn State University Food Science Experiments: www.foodscience.psu.edu/outreach/fun_food_science.html (grades K–12)
Offers a thorough list of links to online curriculum guides, experiments, and other materials related to the science of foods for students, teachers, and parents.

Project Learn: www.ucar.edu/learn/ (educators, grades 6–9)
Offers an online teaching module with an atmospheric cycles theme. Topics include climate, the greenhouse effect, global climate change, and ozone.

Rader's Biology4Kids: www.biology4kids.com (ages 11–13)
Covers the basics of biology, including microorganisms, animal systems, invertebrates, and vertebrates.

Rader's Chem4Kids: www.chem4kids.com (grades 5–9)
Offers an introduction to the science of chemistry, including information on the periodic table, atoms, reactions, and biochemistry.

Rader's Geography4Kids: www.geography4kids.com (grades 5–9)
Includes information on physical geography and earth science basics such as the atmosphere, hydrosphere, and biosphere.

Teaching Tools

Brainchild Learning Tools: www.brainchild.com (educators, grades K–12)
Offers assessments, products, and software for teachers in math and reading, based on state standards.

Internet4Classrooms: www.internet4classrooms.com (educators, grades K–12)
Offers a variety of links to helpful sites with assessment help, online practice modules, and in-school integration support.

References

Allen, R. (2003, Fall). Embracing math: Attitudes and teaching practices are changing—slowly. *Curriculum Update,* 1–8.

Allen, R. (2004, Summer). Shaking up science: Putting physics first changes more than sequence. *Curriculum Update,* 1.

American Association of Colleges for Teacher Education. (2003). The Third International Mathematics and Science Study (TIMSS) 1999 video study. Available at www.nces.ed.gov/pubs2003/timssvideo (retrieved January 23, 2006).

Armour-Thomas, E. (1992). Mathematical competence and the educationally at risk learner: Implications for assessment. In R. Tobias, (Ed.), *Nurturing at-risk youth in math and science: Curriculum and teaching considerations (A+ practices)* (pp. 121–147). Bloomington, IN: Solution Tree (formerly National Educational Service).

Ashford, E. (2003, July 22). Some states are rethinking exit exam policies. *School Board News, 23*(10), 1–4.

Association for Supervision and Curriculum Development. (1991). *Effective Schools for children at risk.* [Video.] Alexandria, VA: Author.

Association for Supervision and Curriculum Development. (2004a, January). Future forecasts. *Education Update, 46*(1), 8.

Association for Supervision and Curriculum Development. (2004b, January). Leading for learning. *Education Update, 46*(1), 1.

Barrett, E. (1992). Teaching mathematics through context: Unleashing the power of the contextual learner. In R. Tobias (Ed.), *Nurturing at-risk youth in math and science: Curriculum and teaching considerations (A+ practices)* (pp. 48–79). Bloomington, IN: Solution Tree (formerly National Educational Service).

Berger, P. (2003). Rubrics: The soft underbelly of standards. *On Board: New York State School Boards Association, 4*(1), 4.

Bloom, B. (1964). *Stability and change in human characteristics.* New York: Wiley.

Bobbit, F. (1918). *The curriculum.* Boston: Houghton Mifflin.

Bobbit, F. (1924). *How to make a curriculum.* Boston: Houghton Mifflin.

Brian, S. J. (1998). *Funtastic math: Probability.* New York: Scholastic.

Brophy, J. E., & Good, T. L. (1974). *Teacher-student relationships.* New York: Holt, Rinehart, and Winston.

Bruner, J. S. (1960). *The process of education.* New York: Vintage Books.

Carson, B., & Murphey, C. (1990). *Gifted hands.* Grand Rapids, MI: Zondervan.

Cattagni, A., & Farris Westat, E. (2001, May). *Internet access in U. S. public schools and classrooms: 1994–2000* (NCES 2001–071). Washington, DC: U. S. Department of Education, National Center for Education Statistics. Available at nces.ed.gov/pubs2001/2001071.pdf (retrieved September 15, 2006).

Cavanaugh, S. (2006, November 12). Technology helps teachers hone in on student needs. *Education Week, 26,* 10.

Checkley, K. (2001, October). Algebra and activism: Removing the shackles of low expectations; a conversation with Robert P. Moses. *Educational Leadership, 59*(2), 6–11.

Collins, M., & Tamarkin, C. (1982). *Marva Collins' way.* Los Angeles: J. P. Tarcher.

Comer, J. P. (1987). New Haven's school-community connection. *Educational Leadership, 44*(6), 13–16.

Comer, J. P. (1998). Educating poor minority children. *Scientific American, 259*(5), 42–48.

Commission on Excellence in Education (1983). *A nation at risk.* Washington, DC: U.S. Government Printing Office.

Community School District 17 [Brooklyn, New York]. (1995, April). *Sample activities from C. S. D. #17 hands-on science staff development program.* Brooklyn, NY: Board of Education, City of New York.

Cooper, H. M. (1979). Pygmalion grows up: A model for teacher expectation communication and performance influence. *Review of Educational Research, 49*(3), 389–410.

Creswell, J. W. (2002). *Educational research: Planning, conducting, and evaluating quantitative and qualitative research.* Upper Saddle River, NJ: Merrill.

Darling-Hammond, L., & McLaughlin, M. (1995). Policies that support professional development in an era of reform. *Phi Delta Kappan, 76*(8), 597–604.

Eick, C. J., Ware, F. N., & Williams, P. G. (2003, January/February). Coteaching in a science methods course: A situated learning model of becoming a teacher. *Journal of Teacher Education, 54*(1), 74–85.

Elementary and Secondary Act of 1965. (1983). *Digest of Education Statistics, 1983–1984.* Washington, DC: U. S. Government Printing Office.

Ellis, S. S., & Whalen, S. F. (1990). *Cooperative learning: Getting started.* New York: Scholastic.

Evertson, C. H., Emmer, E. T., Clements, B. S., and Worsham, M. E. (1997). *Classroom management for elementary teachers.* Boston: Allyn & Bacon.

Falvey, M. A., Givner, C. C., & Kimm, C. (1995). What is an inclusive school? In R. A. Villa & J. S. Thousand (Eds.), *Creating an inclusive school* (pp. 1–11). Alexandria, VA: Association for Supervision and Curriculum Development.

Florida Department of Education. (1993). *Science for all students: The Florida pre-K–12 science curriculum framework.* Tallahassee, FL: Author.

Fountain, C. A., & Evans, D. B. (1994). Beyond shared rhetoric: A collaborative change model for integrating preservice and inservice urban educational systems. *Journal of Teacher Education, 45*(3), 218–227.

Georgia study shows state-funded pre-K boosts student skills. (2003). *Winning Beginning, 2,* 6. Available at www.winningbeginningny.org/brochure/wbny_news2.pdf (retrieved August 30, 2006).

Glenn, J. M. (2000, November 27). [Memorandum attached to *Before it's too late: A report to the nation from the National Commission on Mathematics and Science Teaching for the 21ˢᵗ Century*]. Washington, DC: U. S. Department of Education.

Good, T. I., & Weinstein, R. G. (1986). *Teacher expectations: A framework for exploring classrooms.* In K. Zomwalt (Ed.), *Improving Teaching* (pp. 63–85). Alexandria, VA: Association for Supervision and Curriculum Development.

Hammrich, P. (2004). *Equity Studies Research Center.* [Leaflet]. New York: City University of New York, Queens College.

Hanson, W., & Graves, B. (1998, February). The visionaries: Creators of worlds. *Government Technology* [online version]. Available at www.govtech.net/magazine/visions/feb98vision/escalante.php (retrieved September 13, 2006).

Hart, B., & Todd, R. R. (2003). The early catastrophe: The 30 million word gap by age 3. *American Educator, 27*(1), pp. 4–9.

Hawkins, D. E., & Vinton, D. A. (1973). *The environmental classroom.* Englewood Cliffs, NJ: Prentice Hall.

Heiser, P. (2004, May 24). Access to technology improving in New York, nation. *On Board: New York State School Boards Association, 5*(9), 7. Available at www.nyssba.org (retrieved September 15, 2006).

Herszenhorn, D. (2006a, May 5). As test-taking grows, test-makers grow rarer. *New York Times,* p. A1.

Herszenhorn, D. (2006b, April 19). New York offers housing subsidy as teacher lure. *New York Times.* Available at www.nytimes.com/2006/04/19/nyregion/19teach.html (retrieved September 15, 2006).

Hollander, S. K. (1977). The effect of questioning on the solution of verbal arithmetic problems. *School Science and Mathematics, 77*(8), 659–661.

Hollander, S. K. (1990). Oral reading accuracy and ability to solve arithmetic word problems. *School Science and Mathematics, 90*(1), 23–27.

Jacobs, H. H. (1989). *Interdisciplinary curriculum: Design and implementation.* Alexandria, VA: Association for Supervision and Curriculum Development.

Jacobs, H. H. (1997). *Mapping the big picture: Integrating curriculum and assessment K–12.* Alexandria, VA: Association for Supervision and Curriculum Development.

Jacobs, H. H. (2001, March). *Designing integrated units with rigor.* Session presented at the Queens High Schools Curriculum Share Fair, Bayside, NY.

Jensen, E. (1998). *Teaching with the brain in mind.* Alexandria, VA: Association for Supervision and Curriculum Development.

Kamii, C., & DeVries, R. (1978). *Physical knowledge in preschool education: Implications of Piaget's theory.* Englewood Cliffs, NJ: Prentice Hall.

Kerrod, R., & Holgate, S. A. (2002). *The way science works: Discover the secrets of science with exciting, accessible experiments.* London: Dorling Kindersley.

Korthagen, F. A. J., & Kessels, J. P. A. M. (1999). Linking theory and practice: Changing the pedagogy of teacher education. *Educational Researcher, 28*(4), 4–17.

Kunjufu, J. (1985). *Countering the conspiracy to destroy black boys.* Chicago: African American Images.

Lawrence-Lightfoot, S. (1978). *Worlds apart: Relationships between families and schools.* New York: Basic Books.

Liaison Committee on the Quality Assurance Program. (1981). *The quality assurance program: A report from the Liaison Committee on the Quality Assurance Program to the North Carolina State Board of Education and the Board of Governors of the University of North Carolina.* Chapel Hill: University of North Carolina.

Lieberman, A. (1995). Practices that support teacher development. *Phi Delta Kappan, 76*(8), 591–596.

Lincoln University, Master of Human Services Program. (2003–2004). *Master's project thesis manual.* Lincoln University, PA: Lincoln University of the Commonwealth System of Higher Education.

Lunenburg, F. C., & Ornstein, A. C. (2004). *Educational administration: Concepts and practices.* Belmont: Wadsworth/Thomson Learning.

Lyons, P., Robbins, A., & Smith, A. (1983). *Involving parents: A handbook for participation in schools.* Ypsilanti, MI: High/Scope Press.

Manouchehri, A. (1998, September/October). Mathematics curriculum reform and teachers: What are the dilemmas? *Journal of Teacher Education, 49*(4), 276–286.

McGee, M. G., & Wilson, D. W. (1984). *Psychology: Science and application.* New York: West Publishing Company.

McGrath, S. (1986). *Fun with physics.* Washington, DC: National Geographic Society.

Miller, S. J. (2000). *Let's fly a kite.* New York: HarperTrophy.

More, R. (2003). Preserving the field experiences of preservice teachers. *Journal of Teacher Education, 54*(1), 31–41.

Moses, R. P., & Charles, C. E., Jr. (2001). *Radical equations: Civil rights from Mississippi to the algebra project.* Boston: Beacon Press.

Musser, G. L., & Burger, W. F. (1991). *Mathematics for elementary teachers: A contemporary approach* (2nd ed.). New York: MacMillan.

Musser, G. L., & Burger, W. F. (1994). *Mathematics for elementary teachers: A contemporary approach* (3rd ed.). New York: MacMillan.

National Assessment of Educational Progress reports significant gains in math scores. (2003, November 25). *School Board News, 23*(17), 1.

National Center for Education Statistics. (1996). Digest of Education Statistics Tables and Figures. Washington, DC: U. S. Department of Education. Available at nces.ed.gov/programs/digest/d96/lt2.asp#c2_6 (retrieved September 15, 2006).

National Commission on Mathematics and Science Teaching for the 21st Century. (2000). *Before it's too late: A report to the nation from the National Commission on Mathematics and Science Teaching for the 21st Century.* Washington, DC: U. S. Department of Education. Available at www.ed.gov/inits/Math/glenn/index.html (retrieved September 15, 2006).

National Council of Teachers of Mathematics. (1989). *Standards for school mathematics.* Reston, VA: Author.

National Research Council. (1993). *National science education standards project.* Washington, DC: National Academy Press.

National School Boards Association (2003, October 14). Errors plague test makers, educators. *School Board News, 23*(14), 8.

New York City Public Schools. (2001–2002). *Annual School Report: New York state and city test results in mathematics.* New York: Queens College School for Math, Science and Technology [Public School 499].

New York City Public Schools (2002). *Early Childhood Literacy Assessment System summary notes.* New York: Queens College School for Math, Science and Technology [Public School 499].

New York City Public Schools. (2002–2003). *Annual School Report: New York state and city test results in mathematics.* New York: Queens College School for Math, Science and Technology [Public School 499].

New York State United Teachers. (2002, December 4). *New York State United Teachers' guide to the New York standards.* Latham, NY: Author.

New York State United Teachers. (2003, November 5). Math-score gains show formula for success. *New York Teacher, 45*(5), 3. Available at: www.nysut.org/newyorkteacher/2003-2004/index.html (retrieved September 15, 2006).

Oakes, J. (1985). *Keeping track: How schools structure inequality.* New Haven, CT: Yale University Press.

Oakes, J. (1990). *Multiplying inequalities: The effects of race, social class, and tracking on opportunities to learn mathematics and science.* Santa Monica, CA: RAND Corporation.

Oakes, J., & Guiton, G. (1995). Matchmaking: The dynamics of high school tracking decisions. *American Educational Research Journal, 32*(1), 3–33.

Onyefulu, I. (1995). *Emeka's gift: An African counting story.* New York: Cobblehill Books.

Organisciak, R., Bologna, R., Bingham, J., Oerhlein, R., Cummings, J., Crocetti, R., Medeiros, R., Moss, T., Demyen, E., Martinez, R., Splendorio, W., Levey, E., & Calder, K. (2003). *School requiring academic progress.* [Report]. Deer Park, NY: Deer Park School District.

Ornstein, A. C., & Hunkins, F. P. (2004). *Curriculum: Foundations, principles and issues.* Boston: Pearson Education/Allyn & Bacon.

Piaget, J. (1967). *Six psychological studies.* New York: Random House.

Reese, C. M., Miller, K. E., Mazzeo, J., & Dossey, J. A. (1997). *NAEP 1996 mathematics report card for the nation and the states.* Washington, DC: U. S. Department of Education, Office of Educational Research and Improvement.

Rendon, L., & Triana, E. M. (1989). *Making mathematics and science work for Hispanics.* Washington, DC: American Association for the Advancement of Science.

Reys, B. J., Reys, R. E., & Chávez, O. (2004). Why mathematics textbooks matter. *Educational Leadership, 61*(5), 61–66.

Ripley, A. (2005). Who says a woman can't be Einstein? *Time, 165*(10), 51.

Rosenthal, R., & Jacobson, L. (1968). *Pygmalion in the classroom: Teacher expectation and pupils' intellectual development.* New York: Holt, Rinehart and Winston.

Rotberg, I. C. (2001). A self-fulfilling prophecy. *Phi Delta Kappan, 83*(2), 170–171.

Russell, M., BeBell, D., O'Dwyer, L., & O'Connor, K. (2003, September/October). Examining teacher technology use: Implication for preservice and inservice teacher preparation. *Journal of Teacher Education, 54*(4), 297–309.

References

Ryan, D. P. (2002, July). *CTB/McGraw-Hill issues: Academic intervention services versus state and corporate secrecy.* Paper presented at a Deer Park, New York, school board meeting concerning inappropriate scoring of the New York State Assessment tests.

Sandberg, B. (2002). Turnaround in math: Bay Shore's remarkable success starts with teamwork, support, training and test analysis. *New York Teacher, 44*(4), 12–13. Available at www.nysut.org/newyorkteacher (retrieved September 15, 2006).

Slaven, R. E., & Madden, N. A. (1989). What works for students at-risk: A research synthesis. *Educational Leadership, 46*(5), 4–12.

Snead, L. C. (1998, September/October). Professional development for middle school mathematics teachers to help to respond to NCTM standards. *Journal of Teacher Education, 4*(4), 287–294.

Sparks, D., & Hirsh, S. (1997). *A new vision for staff development.* Alexandria, VA: Association for Supervision and Curriculum Development.

Swanson, M. L., & Swenson, K. A. (Eds.). (1991). *Student resource handbook: Guide for using mathematics for elementary teachers* (3rd Ed.). New York: MacMillan.

Taba, H. (1962). *Curriculum development: Theory and practice.* New York: Harcourt Brace Jovanovich.

Third International Mathematics and Science (TIMSS) Study. (2003). No common teaching method found. *Briefs, 24*(4), 1. Available through the American Association of Colleges for Teacher Education at www.aacte.org.

Tobias, R. (1989). Educating black urban adolescents: Issues and programs. In R. L. Jones (Ed.), *Black adolescents* (pp. 207–227). Berkeley, CA: Cobb & Henry.

Tobias, R. (1992). *Nurturing at-risk youth in math and science: Curriculum and teaching considerations (A+ practices).* Bloomington: Solution Tree (formerly National Educational Service).

Trager, J. (1979). *The people's chronology: A year-by-year record of human events from prehistory to the present.* New York: Holt Rinehart and Winston.

Tyler, R. W. (1949). *Basic principles of curriculum and instruction.* Chicago: University of Chicago Press.

U. S. Department of Education. (2002, January 8). No child left behind (NCLB). Washington, DC: Author. Available at www.ed.gov/nclb/landing.jhtml?src-pb (retrieved September 15, 2006).

U. S. Department of Health, Education and Welfare, Office of Child Development. (1975). *Head Start performance standards* (OCD Notice N–30–36414). Washington, DC: Government Printing Office.

Van Scotter, R. D., Kraft, R. J., & Hass, J. D. (1979). *Foundations of education: Social perspectives.* Englewood Cliffs, NJ: Prentice-Hall.

Wadsworth, B. J. (1996). Piaget's theory of cognitive and affective development. In A. W. Hoy (Ed.), *Educational psychology* (2004, 9th Ed.), (pp. 28–39). Boston: Allyn & Bacon.

Welner, K., & Oakes, J. (1996). (Li)Ability grouping: The new susceptibility of school tracking systems to legal challenges. *Harvard Educational Review, 66*(3), 451–470.

Willis, S. (1995a, Summer). Reinventing science education: Reformers promote hands on, inquiry-based learning. *Curriculum Update,* 1–5.

Willis, S. (1995b). Teachers as researchers: Educators use action research to improve practices. *Education Update 37*(3), 1–4.

Wilson, E. O. (2002). The power of storytelling. *American Educator, 26*(1), 8–11.

Wolf, S., Carey, A., & Mieras, E. L. (1996). "What is this literachurch stuff anyway?" Preservice teachers' growth in understanding children's literary response. *Reading Research Quarterly, 31*(2), 130–157.

Make the Most of Your
Professional Development Investment

Let Solution Tree (formerly National Educational Service) schedule time for you and your staff with leading practitioners in the areas of:

- **Professional Learning Communities** with Richard DuFour, Robert Eaker, Rebecca DuFour, and associates
- **Effective Schools** with associates of Larry Lezotte
- **Assessment *for* Learning** with Rick Stiggins and associates
- **Crisis Management and Response** with Cheri Lovre
- **Classroom Management** with Lee Canter and associates
- **Discipline With Dignity** with Richard Curwin and Allen Mendler
- **PASSport to Success** (parental involvement) with Vickie Burt
- **Peacemakers** (violence prevention) with Jeremy Shapiro

Additional presentations are available in the following areas:

- At-Risk Youth Issues
- Bullying Prevention/Teasing and Harassment
- Team Building and Collaborative Teams
- Data Collection and Analysis
- Embracing Diversity
- Literacy Development
- Motivating Techniques for Staff and Students

Solution Tree

304 West Kirkwood Avenue
Bloomington, IN 47404
(812) 336-7700
(800) 733-6786 (toll free)
FAX (812) 336-7790
email: info@solution-tree.com
www.solution-tree.com

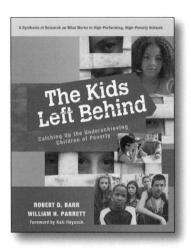

The Kids Left Behind
Robert D. Barr and William H. Parrett
Successfully reach and teach the underachieving children of poverty with the help of this comprehensive resource.
BKF216

Classroom Management for Academic Success
Lee Canter
This groundbreaking resource details effective management strategies you can implement from day one so that all students achieve in the classroom.
BKF219

Learning by Doing
Richard DuFour, Rebecca DuFour, Robert Eaker, and Thomas Many
Perplexing problems become workable solutions as collaborative teams take action to close the knowing-doing gap and transform their schools into PLCs.
BKF214

The School of Belonging Plan Book
David A. Levine
This plan book helps you build a culture of caring where students feel safe and are nurtured toward achievement.
BKF218

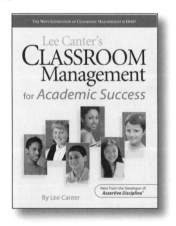